Living Your Best 5D Life

"A brilliant masterpiece full of practical life-changing tools to bring a person into 5D reality now. It is a must-have for every human being on the planet, especially those on a transformational or ascension path. Maureen has given us simple, invaluable, practical guidance to have an extraordinary, expanded, happy life. No more suffering folks! It's all about love! Whether you're a seasoned explorer of consciousness or just beginning your journey, this book is a must-read for anyone seeking to unlock the full potential of their being. It is a true gift for humanity!"

SYLVIA MOSS, VIBRATIONAL SOUND HEALER
AND AUTHOR OF *ANGELS OF NEW YORK*

"A comprehensive and deep exploration of ascension using multidimensional skills. As you discover 5D and learn how to stay in the zone where things go well in life, your encounters with others become more harmonious and loving; you feel blissful and happy. As Maureen says, 'It's available to all who choose to ascend.' She believes you can be an Ascended Master, a human who cocreates reality in 3D with God, by opting out of mass consciousness, elevating yourself way beyond it. Her Bedtime Prayer resonates with God's crystalline light to heal your DNA. This book is enjoyable and great for gentle dimensional shifting. It is time to find your joy!"

BARBARA HAND CLOW, AUTHOR OF
ALCHEMY OF NINE DIMENSIONS

"This is no spiritual bypass book. Readers will receive the unique gift of Maureen St. Germain's revelatory blend of our current sociopolitically imposed illusion with her application of ancient wisdom and galactic context. With her personal, generous, and prescriptive offerings, Maureen opens the door to practical 5D living in the present moment and masterfully equips us, as individuals and as a species, to fully cross the threshold into a liberating and golden transcendence."

LEAH LaCHAPELLE, PERSONAL EVOLUTION COACH
AND 5D MESSENGER

"Maureen has done it again! This book is a powerful, multidimensional, and clarity-provoking guidebook for navigating the changing times."
DANIELLE RAMA HOFFMAN, AUTHOR OF
THE MAGDALENE MANIFESTATION CARDS

"There has never been a better time for a book like this. Maureen J. St. Germain has given us a map to previously uncharted territories. We are approaching a place where dreams and visions can achieve a reality unimaginable in past times. This is not a general outline; what is presented here is a step-by-step process, from MerKaBas to timelines, to achieve the clarity of the life we are meant to live. We are about to become new humans, and this book, far beyond the realm of so many others, gives us the keys to the realization, the awakening, and the activation of the final emergence: the hieros gamos, the sacred marriage of the spirit and the flesh."
ALAN STEINFELD, AUTHOR OF *MAKING CONTACT*

"Dive deep into the realms of possibility with this groundbreaking book that is a transformational experience, a journey of discovery, reality guidance, and illumination for your 5D Being. A life-changing book."
LUMARI, AUTHOR OF *STREAMS OF CONSCIOUSNESS*

"One of the many things I love about this book is that it's a practical how-to book. She writes as if chatting with a friend about accessing the 5D in an accessible, down-to-earth way that removes any barriers to achieving this powerful spiritual work. Bravo, Maureen, and thank you!"
GEORGINA CANNON, AUTHOR OF *THE THIRD CIRCLE PROTOCOL*

"Take time to read *Living Your Best 5D Life*. It sheds light on new experiences the author's clients and students have had along with the fifth-dimensional understanding of what is really going on. She gives you practical tools to not only be in the fifth dimension but to stay in the fifth dimension, without regressing to third-dimension thinking and actioning. The world is becoming fifth-dimensional whether you are ready or not. Join the exodus from third dimension into the fifth dimension—where love is the governing key."
TOM T. MOORE, AUTHOR OF
THE GENTLE WAY SERIES OF BOOKS

Living Your Best 5D Life

TIMELESS TOOLS TO ACHIEVE AND MAINTAIN YOUR NEW REALITY

Maureen J. St. Germain

Bear & Company
Rochester, Vermont

Bear & Company
One Park Street
Rochester, Vermont 05767
www.BearandCompanyBooks.com

Text stock is SFI certified

Bear & Company is a division of Inner Traditions International

Cataloging-in-Publication Data for this title is available from the Library of Congress

ISBN 978-1-59143-531-0 (print)
ISBN 978-1-59143-532-7 (ebook)

Printed and bound in the United States by Lake Book Manufacturing, LLC
The text stock is SFI certified. The Sustainable Forestry Initiative® program promotes sustainable forest management.

10 9 8 7 6 5 4 3 2 1

Text design and layout by Virginia Scott Bowman
This book was typeset in Garamond Premier Pro with Playfair Display used as the display typeface

To send correspondence to the author of this book, mail a first-class letter to the author c/o Inner Traditions • Bear & Company, One Park Street, Rochester, VT 05767, and we will forward the communication, or contact the author directly at **stgermainmysteryschool.com**.

Scan the QR code and save 25% at InnerTraditions.com. Browse over 2,000 titles on spirituality, the occult, ancient mysteries, new science, holistic health, and natural medicine.

This book is a heartfelt tribute to the cherished clients, friends, and partners whose unwavering support has fueled both myself and this endeavor. Through the extraordinary journey into the realm of 5D, we have been enveloped in boundless kindness, creativity, and inspiration.

◆ ◆ ◆

To the esteemed members of the Ascension Institute, Advanced, whose dedication has provided a fertile ground for the insights shared within these pages, I am deeply humbled and grateful. A profound debt of gratitude is owed to the remarkable team at Inner Traditions, whose steadfast support has been instrumental in bringing this latest exploration of 5D to fruition. I extend my heartfelt appreciation to my esteemed editor, Albo Sudekum, whose exceptional guidance has elevated this work to new heights. Special thanks are also extended to the talented individuals within the publicity and design departments whose contributions have been invaluable. Your unwavering commitment to my work is truly appreciated.

◆ ◆ ◆

Love,
Maureen

Contents

Prologue

I've always felt that life has amazing possibilities. I'm just a person, like you, yet with the tools and skills I've learned. I've observed myself and my students doing extraordinary things. I have watched the people I've taught achieve truly life-changing results. And you, dear reader, will you do the same? I have actually learned that we have the power and CAN change the course of where our life is going, and to help others along the way do that as well. Is this your desire?

By now you've heard the statement, "The game is over; the game will end when there are no more players. Will you be the first to leave or the last?"* This book is about the new, amazing game ahead of us. This transformation is a mental and physical exercise that can only be driven by spiritual willingness to shift and change. Your wake-up call helped you recognize your situation. This book will give you more understanding to help motivate you, solid tools to navigate your situation and circumstances—even though you arranged them—and to find your way with joy, grace, and ease!

It will be like nothing you have ever experienced before. Get ready to race to . . . not the finish line, but the starting block! My goal is to help you with new tools, and prepare you for the unexpected and wonderful opportunities that lay ahead of you. I will help you with accessing your inner wisdom and opening to your higher consciousness—a very real part of who you are.

You'll find that other half of you, your inner world, which will

---

*Sanat Kumara—through Maureen J. St. Germain, Hong Kong 2018.

add to every experience, expanding what you can and will do. Let's first start out with a review of some of the tools you'll need.

The spiral chakra is a feminine and balanced way of activating the chakras. Their expanding outward starts to collect information at a whole new level. This meditation was taught in my previous book, *Mastering Your 5D Self*. It's also available on my Illuminate app.* In this meditation, each of you will find out how long you can keep your outer chakras spinning around you. Many will activate them and then pull them back in after experiencing the letting out into the rotation around you. Remember, the chakras were never intended to be locked in the body, but to be a true outward system to collect the cosmic information you may be getting. I highly recommend you acquire the much-needed practice of spiraling your chakras. It will open a new gateway of knowledge for you.

Throughout this book you will find references to my recorded meditations. These will be marked by a diamond ◆ and accompanied by a representative prayer plus a key takeaway to help you choose which meditation you'd like to explore.

In this book I will also encourage you to activate your five Secret Ray Chakras in order to connect with the five Secret-Ray Elohim. The five Secret-Ray Elohim are not known by name, yet we know they exist and are part of the support system that was arranged for us as a way to achieve our personal mastery. Whether you are Hindu or Muslim or Buddhist or Christian or any other belief or persuasion, the perfect human consciousness energy of the perfected human is the same for everyone. I use the convenient name of Christ Consciousness. Because the Elohim are secret, their names are unknown, and we can call them by this name.

---

*Maureen's Illuminate app is available on iPhone or Android.

There is great value in working with the Secret Ray Chakras. They were secret chakras for a very long time, because humanity wasn't ready for their energy, nor were they understood clearly. The locations of the Secret Ray Chakras are on the palms of the hand and the soles of the feet, along with the spleen. Many new tools and dispensations have been brought forward and are just waiting for the time when you are ready and willing to intentionally activate. Now is the time to activate your Secret Ray Chakras.

Who are the Dhyani Buddhas and who are their cohorts, and what does this mean for you? The Maha Chohan leads our list as the representative of the father/mother/spirit God. Beloved Mighty Cosmos, according to the book *The Masters and Their Retreats* by Mark and Elizabeth Prophet, is a being whose, energies for initiation in the mysteries of the Christos. This means, you can just ask him to assists you in bringing in all the fabulous energy that hasn't been available to you to access! This gives you entrée to primary Masters that hold this energy. In addition, the five Secret Rays are providing energy and support for you to embody these wonderful qualities that are represented by the Secret-Ray Elohim and the 5D Dhyani Buddhas.

We call to the Five Dhyani Buddhas clear out the human poisons and activate anger and hate and hate creation; greed; jealousy; spiritual, intellectual, and human pride; all cravings, covetousness, greed, and lust; fear and doubt. This meditation takes only five minutes, and activates these powerful externally based chakras. There is great value in working with the Secret Ray Chakras. They were secret for a very long time because humanity wasn't ready for their energy, nor were they understood clearly. The locations of the Secret Ray Chakras are on the palms of the hand and the soles of the feet along with the spleen. In the world, many new tools and dispensations have been brought forward and are just waiting for the time when you are ready and willing to intentionally activate. This is the time to activate your Secret Ray Chakras. More on that at the end of this chapter and in chapter 11.

It is my deep pleasure to welcome you into this magical world. Remember, you may have access to more than one dimension because you are becoming multidimensional. You may be surprised or confused about what is happening and may be thinking there is something wrong with you. This book, the third in my series on the 5th Dimension, will help guide you.

THE EMPATHY RESPONSE

You will learn new ways to ramp up your thoughts and communications to express the empathy response. It will help you understand and master your own circumstances and understand more of the world around you. Technology on Earth has raced ahead of Spirituality. It's time for your spirituality to catch up. This book provides understanding, validation, and tools to assist you in achieving this leveling up that is necessary to the balance the technology. Together we will address practical elements such as concerns about the electrification of the planet, along with creating awareness of how you can work around this and all kinds of unseen toxicity in and around you! A new meditation, the Spiral Chakra Meditation, is included that addresses this issue. You will also find insights to empower you to know and understand the rapid evolution humanity is slated for.

This book also releases the new 8D MerKaBa Meditation, which is based on the capacity to exceed the speed of light, an esoteric hidden mystery channeled by Source. This is in alignment with the true nature and progression of the human.

The following chapters will identify events and activities you may experience or may be experiencing that will allow you to know you are actively in 5D. This will help you self-evaluate and to move forward with grace and ease. How do you connect the dots? By truly embracing the idea that reality is changing so dramatically, it has become almost unrecognizable!

···1···

Making 5D Work
Every Day

The arrival of the new era of the 5th Dimension has confused many people and made many awakened people live more in the present. When we wake up, it is not for us to be warriors, it is not for us to deny the past, but for us to be more connected with ourselves, to use our energy and strength more for bringing ourselves into so much alignment that our irresistible presence invites cooperation and kindness.

The quality of more awareness, our higher nature, and more respect for our Earth and every one of its people takes us into our galactic citizenship. Chi is the carrier of all things. Chi orchestrates everything! It regulates blood, digestion, and everything behind the scenes—all the involuntary actions of the body. When we activate chi, and imbue it with our love and appreciation for all of life, we are 5th-Dimensional creatures. Less thinking gives way to more energy for flowing, joyful expression. Doing LESS allows us to do more! Consider taking up the martial art of Qigong (pronounced chi-gong) to elevate your physical expression along with your spiritual expression.

What is 5D (5th Dimension)? Experiences when everything goes well, interactions are harmonious and loving, and all feels blissful and happy—that's 5D. It's a vibratory zone that carries with it the God consciousness, where love is the governing rule—and it's available to all who choose to ascend. Being in 5D is a frequency choice; it's about using what's available to assist you when you fall out of higher frequencies. Being there doesn't guarantee you'll stay there. Certainly, once you've been there it becomes easier and easier to get back to. And when you go there frequently, it becomes easier and easier to stay for longer periods, until your need to slide back into 3D evaporates. Even though you'll hear me say it's a bit like "heaven," you don't go there and stay, nor do you lose your body! Instead, like a sine wave, you'll slide into 5D and back to 3D regularly, until you don't! Those who read my book *Waking Up in 5D* will remember the explanation for why we don't dwell in the 4th Dimension. 4D is a transitional place, not a place for our ascension. Furthermore, 4th Dimension vibrates faster than 3rd dimension; it is more potent than 3rd dimension. It still carries polarity, which means the lower 4D has lots of entities of the kind you will not want to associate with.

Have you ever lost your taste for something you used to enjoy? Leaving 3D is a bit like that. At one time, we thoroughly enjoyed the expansion of the physical nature of reality. We enjoyed creating so many wonderful things in 3D. Today, though, 3D has devolved enough for the return to a new cycle toward Source. Do you still perhaps yearn for a few things you enjoyed as a child; but, for the most part, being an adult is what you yearned for as a child. As an adult, now you yearn for mastery.

Do you know how to live your life as a 5D being?

Where will you get your intel? How will you focus on being and staying 5D, since life keeps bringing up more distractions or challenges to overcome? This is a sweet and fun subject to write about because I believe when we get more challenges to our 5D expression, we are honing and perfecting our work. Think of a professional ball player. He or she doesn't stop practicing their game as long as they are a player of the game. Our efforts improve with daily practice, so your first step is to have a daily practice. Read more about daily practice in chapter 7.

How will you know what you need to know? Go to the songs that have sent messages for so long. For example, listen to the old song by Jackson Browne *Doctor My Eyes*. If you listen to any popular music, you may find it full of uplifting messages. Focus on those! The same can be said for social media and movies. You may choose what you expose your mind and body to. Make the commitment to choose uplifting influences.

In certain Tibetan meditation techniques, they recognize that understanding and wisdom are indeed necessary in order to understand the deepening information that can be forthcoming through meditation, or through the Akashic Records. There is a buddha called Manjushree, who assists with separating ignorance. Vairochana is a Tibetan buddha who assists you by stamping out ignorance to make room for wisdom and understanding. Learning to connect the dots is a mix of wisdom and understanding as applied to tolerance and compassion. Manjushree holds a sword to cut through stubborn belief systems in order to help you live in a place of harmony with your current situation, while allowing you to adopt effective behaviors that lead to a meaningful life. You can call upon Manjushree to help you cut through the veil of ignorance, false beliefs, and thoughtforms that control you. Practicing the six-minute Five Dhyani Buddhas Meditation* will also free you from outside influences.

Let's identify events and activities you may experience or may be experiencing that will allow you to know you are actively in 5D. Here's how to self-evaluate and move forward with grace and ease: You may feel normal, but things just don't add up. The unexplainable happens to you regularly. You start to read about 5D, and suddenly the light comes on! You have changed vibrationally, affecting everything around you. You find humor in everything you encounter and your joy is high. There is no going back. Welcome to your new home!

Connecting the dots in 5D means you are ready and willing to abandon old ways of doing life and are open to being so compassionate toward anything and everything that nothing bothers you. When everyday drama makes you laugh—not at others, but at the absurdity of 3D life from a 5D perspective—that's confirmation you are in 5D. There are other ways to know you are in 5D, which you will learn in this book.

RIGHT ANGLE

In this section I'd like to point out that the right-angle turn seems to be an important part of the dimensional shift mysteries. Magnetic energy is receptive and electric energy is advancing. These two opposing and pulling energies are at right angles to each other in an electrical system. Energy moves the same way. This ninety-degree turn pulls you forward into a dimensional shift. Understanding this right-angle turn means you are making a complete departure from the reality you know and are familiar with, to a version that feels like there is no connection to your present. The Hathors tell us, through Tom Kenyon, that fear is the number-one way humanity is controlled. To the human, fear of the unknown is very real. So, not to discount this, but when one exists in a 3rd- or 4th-Dimensional reality, fear is real. Why? Because one believes it. When you are in a complete state of calm, it's like you are in the eye of a storm. Nothing can touch you.

One other thing the right angle produces is its affinity to phi. For example, the Golden Mean rectangle is created by the relationship of phi (one edge multiplied by 1.618, or phi, to create the long edge) to the 90-degree turn created to produce the rectangle.

Now, there will come a "time" when separation of dimensions no longer matters. When they are no longer separated, your awareness knows that technically they do not exist. They were separated so that one could come to understand them, to transcend them, and to no longer need to see them separately. REMEMBER, *separation* is a creation we agreed to. When you release this human need to separate, you will no longer care about this, nor see separation as real. Yet, inside the matrix, inside the illusion, inside the physical aspect of the hologram, your perception is that of separation. The prime directive when leaving Source was indeed to separate. And this book is written for those who still exist (even if part time) inside the hologram, for, again, once you do not, you will be in a place of non-duality.

REMINDER: If you believe it, it is real. The key to 5D is to challenge what you have believed, in order to make room for a new belief system and new expression in your reality.

It's time. It's time to move into your place of unconditional love. Life on this planet can be strange and unpredictable. You may face many crazy events in the next few months or years. You will learn to hold your own and stay connected to your heart. At the start of 2020–21, I devised a basic countdown to help us avoid succumbing to fear. Since then, I've rerecorded it so it's even easier to move into a heart space, and I do the counting for you! Sometimes all you need is for someone to talk you off the ledge. It's called the Seven Archangels and the Wheel Meditation.* I've included it here, but of course it's lovely to listen on my Illuminate app.

Seven Archangels and the Wheel Meditation

Archangel Uriel, assist me with materializing my divine plan.
Bring harmony between my awareness and the reality
and the ideal.

A key takeaway from the Seven Archangels and the Wheel Meditation: This effective guided meditation takes you through the seven Archangels in a very powerful and unique way. Ever think of just one more thing after you've submitted a response to a question? Me too! This meditation is unique because it helps you focus and then gives you that second chance. First the seven Archangels' gifts are highlighted, and you are shown how you can benefit from their gifts and their ability to help you clear your history, and then become your most evolved self. And finally, like a Ferris wheel, go around the wheel one more time, this time loading up new and special gifts to help you be proactive. You'll come away from this meditation a new and unique you, ready for the new Millennium.

✳

This is a good time to be reminded of the value of two of my favorite tools for helping you stay in 5th Dimension. The first is to repeat this phrase at least once daily: "I am asking for a day of heaven on Earth, for me and everyone I'm in contact with, and everyone I am in contract with!" This key phrase will change everything for you, and will improve communications with everyone you talk to! My other favorite tool is to announce, when going to sleep: "I am waking up in 5D." This announcement to yourself and your Angels and Guides sets your intention for the day to come.

Back in the '90s, I asked my Angels and Guides why I couldn't just announce "I'm in" for the rest of my life. Why did I have to go to all the trouble of inviting them in every day, and asking for their help every day! They replied, "Well, honey, when we got married ten years ago, I told you that I love you, and nothing has changed." I burst out laughing! I KNEW that when in relationship, you tell your beloved "I love you" every day. When this doesn't occur, you know you are in trouble, or you or your partner is sick or isn't feeling well.

I began to understand that choosing every day was an important part of living! The Angels showed me the sunrise through sunset, and indicated that EVERY DAY we get a clean slate. Each day we must determine who or what we are aligned with. We get to select who we love, what we will do, how we will change, when we will do it, and where. We get to find the resources, the tools, and the opportunities to make the magic happen—and we get to ask for help.

We might be going through a rough patch and need extra support. We often forget how much we are loved by Source! Can you start your habit of connecting with the Angels or the Ascended Masters today? It may be that you've never asked for help because you don't believe in them. Surprisingly, that doesn't even matter! My experience has shown otherwise. My students have filled my journals with their stories of how they have almost nonchalantly asked for help because they liked me, or they thought maybe there was something to this . . . and voilà, magic happens.

Take for example Brandon, a member of my monthly online study group "St. Germain's Ascension Portal," who is a juggler of deals and needed a number of different participants to agree in order to make his latest project a go. Things were falling apart until he saw my blog post about the Golden Sheets* and wondered, "What the heck, let me read her post and see what all the fuss is about." He'd read about the Golden Sheets before, but had dismissed them in his mind. This time, he couldn't WAIT to report to the members of the Ascension Portal. As soon as he asked for assistance from the Golden Sheets, the whole deal fell into place like a puzzle, and then some—there were bonuses and side deals that also added to the total outcome of his project!

The Open Your Heart to Love Countdown Meditation* was created to make it easier to get into your heart and to exercise your heart muscle. Sometimes we are so filled with fear and worry that it is hard to concentrate on anything else. This meditation will lift your spirits and leave you feeling enriched by the presence of your Higher Self, firmly anchored in your heart. Some people have said this is their very favorite meditation.

Open Your Heart to Love Countdown Meditation

I ask Source to help me open my heart to receiving
and giving love!

A key takeaway from the Open Your Heart to Love Countdown Meditation: If you've wanted to find a way to be more open-hearted, this meditation is an ideal choice! It is soothing, inspiring, and sweet. In this meditation, count backward from ten to get into the heart, then connect with the heart. When you've done that, count forward to ten, reclaiming energies that fill you.

If you've ever felt like your Higher Self connection needed a boost, this meditation, when used on a regular basis, will assist in creating that space and awareness of your Higher Self. I hope you enjoy it!

---

*From July 2022.

···2···
5D Tools for Transforming Your Environment

What tools do you have? What tools can you use? When you think about the words listed in my book *Waking Up in 5D*—"I have to," "I should," etc.—have you replaced them with a new pattern? How about letting yourself own your actions instead of "passing blame." Or passing shame? Don't let anyone distract the conversation away from the change you know you need to make!

What is a distraction from the real conversation?

1. A polarized perspective prevents you from finding your middle way.
2. Changing how you approach life will help you stay in 5D.
3. Discover awareness and curiosity. Rather than judgment about new and interesting things that may surprise or scare you, consider that curiosity will keep you out of judgment.
4. Try to stay in wonder!
5. What keeps you curious without comparison?
6. Notice that your Higher Self connection will help you to act in the highest way.
7. Find your bliss—maybe it's a song, or maybe an experience like walking in a park or on the beach.
8. Keep smiling. Bless those that hurt you, they need it.

When you are in judgment, you are locked into 3D. This is why, in 5D, if you find you no longer desire to keep track of what others are doing, you can know that you truly don't care—not because you are heartless, but because your love for yourself and others allows for great compassion for each of you! Now you are operating in the new paradigm of 5D. What if you are being accused of something you did not do? If you are offended by the accusation, you are still in 3D and still holding judgment. When you laugh at the accusation, you are in 5D; you are not threatened by someone else's accusation because you don't care whether they believe you or not, and because you are so sure of your own actions, you find what might be an annoying accusation actually amusing! Being in integrity is about being self-aware within yourself, knowing with absolute certainty who you are and at the same time being willing to hear others or your Guides when you need to change.

SYMPTOMS OF APPROACHING THE ASCENSION

Certain ascension symptoms are now presenting in our world. Being aware of them will give you peace of mind, even with the discomfort! Understand that ascension symptoms can be extremely mysterious and hard on the body. A short list is given below that may be helpful in case your doctors cannot find the cause. If you cannot determine the cause of these symptoms through consultation with traditional doctors or alternative healers, consider that they may be coming from the many upgrades you may be getting in your body. Your health care professional is an important first line of action when encountering any health issue, but humanity is developing a crystalline base. Remember that your physical body will become the Ascended Master You. You will not need to die to make this happen.

Ascension symptoms can include headaches due to the expansion of your pineal gland. Your brain may feel like the cranium is too small. You may experience vertigo, dizziness, forgetfulness, joint and body pain or aches, cramps in your legs, or changes in your sight and in your awareness of your immediate space. You may feel feverish or flu-like symptoms, cramps and diarrhea, or even kundalini experiences. This may result in anxiety attacks that come and go quickly. Activating the Kundalini prematurely can also cause major health issues. Many of these upgrades can occur at night, and you might wake up for "no reason" and decide to use the bathroom. This is often a signal that you are "giving permission" to whatever upgrade the benevolent ETs of the light may be assisting you with. Announcing "I am waking up well rested no matter what the night holds" will also ease this transformation.

Remember that you, as a vessel of light, are being upgraded in many ways. Humanity has chosen this path, albeit painful. One way to address this is to notice it is happening, and to say the following prayer:

I ask that this divine upgrade assist me and allow me to pursue my highest purpose in this lifetime with the most evolved appearance possible and expressing in the kindest, most generous and gentle way. Amen.

Self-care of the physical body is your highest priority right now. Massage, body work, craniosacral work, long baths, etc., will do much for the integration of this new evolved energy. You are becoming 5th-Dimensional. Seek not to understand, but to integrate it with grace and ease.

Your hearing structures are going to be rewired. This has caused some of you to start hearing extra ordinary things, which most people do not hear. This can include Wi-Fi or light. Some of you can hear "light." Some of you can hear the screeching of Wi-Fi. Your perceptions are growing, yet in the field of 3D they may seem painful or annoying, at best. You know that there is more "light" on the planet for each of us to experience. As you bring it into your own body, it will take considerable effort to allow these experiences to become your new normal. Your physical body is learning to be the Ascended Master You. This involves accepting more light into your every activity, and especially into your physical body!

In 3D we have memory, which allows us to compare or to possibly judge. In higher dimensions there is no memory; there is no need to keep track of others or ourself. It doesn't mean you won't remember; it means when you need a memory you will easily pull it in from the Akashic Records. Some of you may be feeling thankful to hear that your memory loss is not due to aging as much as it is to the shifting of dimensions!

Once you start spending more time in the higher dimensions, the things you experience there are not as well remembered. In 3D, memory serves to anchor us there. In 4D, a vast vibrational location, there are low areas that will pull you down, but you'll also find that, in the higher realms of 4D (very, very close to 5D), the *past and future* begin to merge. You are operating more from the standpoint of being in the present, so therefore there's really no need for memory. As you move into the higher dimensions, there is no memory, as the unfolding is spontaneous. The unfolding of memory becomes "on demand." One of my students, Kelly, reminded me that this concept took a bit of deep thinking, and you may want to sit with it too.

She even wrote, "Since the workshop, when I look back at some of my notes, I marvel at the fact that I do not 'remember' writing most of them! But it's a rather new experience of recalling instead of remembering . . . the only way I can explain it is, it's like when you know there is something saved on your computer, but you don't remember what it is called or what it was about . . . but something (an innate knowing of sorts) will trigger the need to restore saved (but not remembered) information and then somehow you bring up the "file" you wanted to recall. Wow, just writing this is enough to make me dizzy!"

You will let go of a certain "density" or denseness in your physical body as it becomes lighter. The crazy thing about this is that the less heavy your cells and vibration become, the more your physical body may resist this lightness. This means your body will try to compensate by resisting, becoming more of a couch potato and gaining weight! There is more to this. The more light you bring in, the more physical exercise is needed. The higher frequency energy can create stress on your nerves, and physical activity balances that! Tools to help you deal with this nervous energy can be the herb Lion's Mane or the Transfusion from God Meditation.*

A key takeaway from this meditation is: I have often wondered how you can create the energy or request you need when you are just so "down" you don't feel like finding the time or energy to ask for help. My imagination showed me that a direct transfusion from Source was like a jet that refuels in midair, like the KC-135 Stratotanker and its iterations.

Transfusion from God Meditation
I claim and accept my Divine Transfusion from Source,
right here, right now.

The only way to deal with this is to allow more spiritual mass into your body by doing more physical activities, such as walking, exercising, running, and swimming. The more physically demanding, the better. Even weight training will be helpful as you spiritually advance. If you can, find a way to spend a good portion of this exercise time outside. Remember, you are becoming 5th-Dimensional from the inside out, producing a crystalline body that can transcend 3rd Dimension into 5th Dimension.

✳

As you grow and shift into the new 5D human, you are stepping into your power as a cocreator shaping your reality in profound ways. Understanding how you will accomplish this is the subject of this book. Everything you create in your world has the opportunity to grow and change. However, you will still need a framework to understand it. Creation doesn't occur in isolation. Imagine trying to create within a void—it's impossible. Boundaries provide that essential contrast, but they're not synonymous with polarity. This book will help you understand that everything you do today affects the past and the future!

Humanity is going through countless shifts and upgrades. I have experienced tangible evidence with clients of dimensional shifts that define a person stepping into an upgrade that allows them to shift instantly, without going through the hard work of the old evolutionary process known in 3D. You'll learn more about this in chapter 4.

My two earlier books, *Mastering Your 5D Self* and *Waking Up in 5D*, have set the stage. This is the opportunity to build on those books and take your ascension work to another level. This book shows you important and necessary steps to accelerate and improve your process into a fully integrated Ascended Master system works, which is radically different from the old patterns.

Humans tend to attribute blame to others for their own problems. Maintaining a positive image, often referred to as "saving face," is a common practice in Chinese culture to uphold one's reputation. However, we need to navigate through the pervasive victim mentality that plagues humanity. Each person possesses the inner strength to overcome defensiveness and embrace growth. Approaching life's challenges with love enables us to accept necessary feedback without succumbing to victimhood. Just as in a board game, losing doesn't mean carrying those setbacks forward. Deep-seated wounds demand focused attention to elevate our consciousness and remain in higher states like 5D.

What if you have arrived, are no longer a victim, are and treated well? How will you validate the wrongdoing done to you? Even if you have done your forgiveness work, you may reverse the energy, feeling superior: "I've arrived, I deserve this. I am entitled to superior treatment." This is still a form of *abuse of power*. It is very easy to fall into abuse of power (ergo the lack of compassion) and the "irritation" is a direct result of feeling superior. Most of you are very compassionate and do not act irritated in normal situations. So why could this happen now?

The answer lies in the concept "When I am in power, I'll (finally) be treated like the queen that I am!" Thing is, no one else knows you are a queen. You have to act like a queen! How do queens act? Well, the good ones are charming and nice, patient and kind. They have great compassion for everyone around them. They reign, not rule. Others will know you are a good queen because of your compassion (your new normal), your considerateness, your gracefulness, and gratefulness for the amazing life you now have. Let's make your life amazing now!

The Transformation
of Beliefs

Think about when you self-criticize. Are you afraid you might appear to be less than perfect? Are you roleplaying using the voice of an early caregiver? We've all encountered some version of this. Where did it come from? Perhaps, as children, when an authority asked, "Did you do this?" our response was "No" because we were afraid we might get in trouble or be punished in some way. As adults there rarely is punishment for our mistakes, yet why must we fear the obvious truth? We must conquer our own fear of not being perfect. Then we will discover that the universe gives us many opportunities, many ways to do things over again. Like the movie *Groundhog Day*, if you don't get it the first time, you'll probably do it again. In 5th Dimension, we try many ways, abandon what is unpleasant, and seek what is pleasing and keep exploring. No need to judge here.

What has happened in your life to make you feel the need to protect yourself, and to keep your foibles from being discovered? I think sometimes the Western culture has trained children to lie because mothers and fathers ask questions they already know the answers to! For example, if the child didn't do their homework, but are scared of the repercussions, they will lie. If they broke something, and it is obvious, perhaps figuring how to fix it, replace it, or do without would be more productive. Everyone has occurrences in life to stimulate the need to be perfect. When you are angry or disappointed in others you depend on, it's challenging to communicate a higher standard without being critical of the past. Whether with your boss or best friend, use these opportunities to raise your consciousness to humility and service. It isn't always easy, but it is part of becoming the Ascended Master You.

When I still worked in the nonprofit world, I came home very angry one evening because I was being blamed for something I thought I was innocent of. I remember complaining at the altar, "I thought you were protecting me." I wailed at El Morya, my spiritual teacher at the time, who is the Master of the Ray of the Will of God. And then I said, "If there was something here for me to learn, I didn't get it. And I'm going to have to do it over again!"

Honestly, I don't recommend you ever speak to your Guides so irreverently, like I did. I hope you laughed when you read that I did. The next day, I was confronted by an even higher authority within my organization. He was very kind, but firm.

"You going to fix this?" he asked, after pointing out my unacceptable behavior.

"Yes," was all I could get out.

He then added, "I won't say anything to your boss about this." (Meaning she won't have cause to fire me!) And then I went home and thanked the El Morya for being so very gentle with me!

You may have learned how damaging and degrading negative self-talk can be, but how do you stop it? Ask your Angels and Guides to alert you when you are doing it, and immediately replace it with a positive version of the same observation. "Gosh, I can be so stupid" becomes "I'm always thinking, saying, and doing intelligent things!" Other writers have written about how to fix negative self-talk, but my emphasis here is more about the premise that what we say matters—sometimes incredibly so.

How do you self-evaluate and move forward with grace and ease? The answer to this question lies in the choice to fix yourself and move toward improvement. Have you found yourself arguing with a friend or loved one when they accuse you of a certain behavior? Are you ready with your defensiveness, to explain that it was the other person's fault? That's the signal that you need to do some serious cleanup work. What if you don't have any of those difficult conversations? You can still ask your Angels and Guides to show you what needs fixing. Wouldn't it be wonderful for all of your relationships if you were able to approach them, without them prompting you, and say, "I think you are right." When you can laugh at the absurdity of all difficult situations, then you've landed in 5D.

CREATION IN THE VOID

You may have been told that the universe is expanding infinitely, yet that is simply not true! The universe is creating and expanding, true, but not infinitely! Why? Because you need a boundary in order to create. The universe may take the next stage of creation into 5D into a whole new creation realm, and it too will have a boundary. Consider this: although there is no science to support a curved universe, according to a study published in *Nature Astronomy* (11/1019) by University of Manchester cosmologist Eleonora Di Valentino, Sapienza University of Rome cosmologist Alessandro Melchiorri, and Johns Hopkins University cosmologist Joseph Silk, "Everything we think we know about the shape of the universe could be wrong. Instead of being flat like a bedsheet, our universe may be curved, like a massive, inflated balloon." What does this mean? That perhaps indeed there is a boundary science has yet to discover.

Why is this important? You are becoming a cocreator and stepping into a powerful role as actualizer of your reality. You may think you need only your ideas, but you need more than that. You need your palette and your canvas. That palette represents your new beliefs, and the canvas can be clear and clean but it still has an outside edge! That is what this book is about. You cannot create in a void. Try to imagine it. It's not possible. How do you measure change in the void? Everything would change with it, there's no point of before and after, no point of start and finish. All of creation needs a boundary. That boundary creates the region between "everything" and possibility/probability. Within the universe, nothing can self-identify or exist without a point of contrast. That original contrast is produced by the boundary. But a boundary is not polarity.

Understanding why we ask "why" leads to self-discovery. We ask "why" because we want to solve the problem at hand. We logically infer that if we know why, we can then come to a solution with our ego or intellect. "Why" is the reason to act. However, "why" distracts you from the flow. Why? It presumes you can solve the problem with your intellect or your mind. In 5D, you get to construct the drama, situation, or concept, and when you run into a roadblock, you consult the universe, allowing it to handle the solving. Announce, "I know there's a solution to this "blank" issue, and I expect the universe to show this to me (if the issue is urgent, add: "And I need it by morning!"). When you create space, creativity will follow.

"Go to the solution or outcome you need. This is why you don't need to see how it will work out! Let the universe deliver to you the fastest solution, and see just how magical it can be."
MAUREEN ST. GERMAIN

"Always think of what you have to do as easy, and it will become so."
ÉMILE COUÉ

How do you speak to yourself when you are accused of being less than perfect? Can you accept that you are not yet perfect? Probably. But, in your defense, you probably have an excuse! This is why, in *Mastering Your 5D Self*, I said that you don't have to say you're sorry! But what about when you regret a past event? The Reality Remix Meditation* will guide you through a process that ensures you can change the past, which will change the future! What does this meditation do? It allows you to create a new version of the scenario, and to then burn that into your psyche so the new, improved version overrides the old one. It changes who you are today, and clears out the regret! You will actually feel lighter.

Reality Remix Meditation
....

I am poised and insightful, prepared to reshape the regretful event by embracing my potent capacity to craft a more favorable past. I firmly envision the new outcome, anchoring it in my reality eternally.

A key takeaway from the Reality Remix Meditation: You may have situations in your life that you realize in hindsight you could have done better! You can set the stage, changing the timeline to one that pleases you, where you actually made the wise choice you now know you could have.

✳

Your self-judgment is yours—you don't need to impress it upon anyone else. Release the things that make you defensive and examine them for what they really are—your own denial of your own inner judgment. Instead dwelling on self-judgment, allow yourself to imagine what the other person's needs are and attempt to support that. Reflect on another's need rather than your own defense.

Is there a part of you that STILL is acting out like the victim? Certainly, in the past you may have been wounded by others but you do not need to be a victim anymore. You do not need to carry those wounds into the new you. You can detach, and staying in 5D is dependent upon that!

Alternate timelines get created when you have guilt or shame. When a random memory comes up that is all about an unsettling event, this is your opportunity to clear and merge it into your present, evolved timeline. One super-fast way to do this is to use the AroMandalas Octa essential oil blend to clear the shame and undo your link to timelines that don't please you. Discover that both shame and irritation are perversions of time! Chapter 6 provides an in-depth discussion of time, so we will pursue this discussion further there. For example, when you say, "I would do it this way . . ." you are implying your way is better. Again, these are ways to deflect, instead of dealing with the cause of the issue, which generally is YOUR resistance to change.

Shame is the false belief that you **could have** done better. Irritation is the false belief that you **would do** it better. For example, "I would do it this way . . ." implying your way is better.

Being a victim allows you to validate the wrongdoing that was done to you. Initially, the desire to be validated comes from missing Source. You've come a long way and are eager for the connection you had when you were with Source. We seek validation because we don't have our connection to Source, so we desire someone else to validate what we went through! How will you validate the wrongdoing done to you? Even if you have done your forgiveness work, you may reverse the energy, feeling superior, "I've arrived, I deserve this. I am entitled to superior treatment."

This is a form of *abuse of power*. It is very easy to fall into abuse of power (ergo the lack of compassion), and the "irritation" is a direct result of feeling superior. Most of you reading this are a very compassionate, and do not act irritated in normal situations. So why would this happen?

Remember, you can choose to embody the essence of royalty! Make this your passion: to show charm, kindness, patience, and benevolence. Your reign as a benevolent leader and royal is evident through your compassion, newfound normalcy, thoughtfulness, tolerance toward others, as well as your elegance and gratitude for the splendid life you presently enjoy

In 5D there is no right or wrong! It's the end of "who's right." It's the end of punishment if you are "wrong"! Our society is advanced enough to find other ways to deal with problems. Humanity is ready to work on both ends, using education and reeducation of the simple values of honesty and integrity and self-determination! But where do we start? We start with ourselves. When you have arrived, and are no longer a victim, you will be 5D.

The universe is being bathed with positive energy that will show up—if you look for it. This energy will support your shifting—when you are willing to let go of the old you, to discover the new inner you, shining brightly. This new self-reflection isn't about ego, but about observation of yourself, so you can support others with willingness not to be apologetic but authentic, to not be shielding but yielding. Find your joy. Anything that is not fun or funny is not in 5D.

These shifts will lead to dimensional shifts like I have seen in others. They are described in the next chapter.

Humanity is moving from a place where you would turn to an expert or Guru, and now must develop your own Inner Guru. The easiest way to do this is to connect with your Higher Self and learn, then choose to follow your Higher Self's information. Developing a good Higher Self connection is imperative. This is not just about trusting your heart or trusting your "gut." It's about building your Higher Self connections with six weeks of important practice, so you don't need to trust your Higher Self—you KNOW your Higher Self. This protocol is in all of my books, and also now on my Illuminate app.

Many times, your Higher Self connection will seem counterintuitive. Many times, you may tell yourself, "No, I don't want to do this." However, with an active Higher Self connection, if you really do need or desire an outcome, your Higher Self will insist. How will it insist? It will repeat the instruction. You may respond with disagreement. The Higher Self will insist again. You might again respond with your ego. The third time your Higher Self tells you to take action, you may finally conclude that it's in your best interest to do so. It always is.

This is where you can practice detachment. You know your Higher Self is right. You have belief in the absence of evidence. You do not have to obey your Higher Self. Instead, through an act of will, using your direct sovereignty, you determine it is in your best interest to follow your Higher Self's wisdom. Submission is replaced by sovereignty.

Your Higher Self can assist in your work with other teachers. Your Higher Self has the discernment to help you learn from others and discard what is not a match for you. You no longer need to determine if someone is a "good teacher or bad teacher." You no longer need to reject someone because their ideas are faulty, but to reject the faulty parts while finding what is useful. There are no more degrees of usefulness other than whether it is a match for you now. When you are inclined to explore or experiment in your process, you can check in with your Higher Self.

Your inner and outer world can be filled with questions. I like "What's going on?" And I prefer "What" over "Why." The reason I prefer the former question, "What's going on?" is because it leaves the field open to inform you of something you may not have thought of. This opens the door to 5D thinking. Asking "Why" causes one to look for a cause and then to use the mind or intellect to solve a problem. Moving to "What" is an important step toward moving out of judgment.

Stepping out of judgment is extremely difficult, yet, with the help of the Five Dhyani Buddhas Meditation, it will seem effortless. It's a six-minute meditation that can set the stage for inner peace and harmony, and recalibrate your reactions.

Five Dhyani Buddhas Meditation

I call upon the Five Dhyani Buddhas to overshadow me with their mastery and to help me activate my five Secret Ray Chakras, so I can elevate my healing and self-mastery.

A key takeaway from the Five Dhyani Buddhas Meditation: The ability to release typical human foibles such as anger, rage, jealousy, and pride.

GROWING YOUR SPIRITUAL PERCEPTION

Making time for your personal introspection is a new priority. Your inner wisdom channel can be activated while you are going for a walk or performing any other mundane task you find yourself immersed in. Initially, this may be the only way you find time for meditation. Then you might move into silent meditation or stillness meditation. If these do not work, you might move into guided meditation. Both will take you where you want to go. Neither is better. Look at your own self-awareness. Can you sit still for five or ten minutes, dismissing all thoughts as they roll into your awareness? If so, then mindfulness meditation is for you. If you like a guided meditation to take your mind off the constant chatter of your mind, then a guided meditation will be more useful for you. Both will take you where you want to go. You may want to join others who are like-minded, who have similar interests and knowledge that will stimulate you to grow and evolve.

Learning to respect others who are dissimilar in belief, yet share common interests, is the first step in moving toward nonjudgmental behaviors. If you have time, volunteering is a powerful community building process. If you have money, your ability to financially support others will make a difference. Put yourself into a willingness to try new things, even if you are a little uncomfortable. This is where real growth occurs, because it will push you out of your comfort zone, where you will need to be honest about what you are capable of and what you are "new" at. Be willing to learn from others, as well as to teach others.

··· 4 ···

Changing the Paradigm

Humanity is going through countless shifts and upgrades. I have experienced tangible evidence with clients, of their dimensional shifts. These are defining events indicating that a person is stepping into an "upgrade" that allows them to shift instantly, without going through the "hard work" of the old evolutionary process known in 3D.

My earlier book, *Waking Up in 5D*, set the stage. This is the "acting class" that shows you how the new system works, which is radically different from old patterns. You can and will experience dimensional shifts as you merge multiple timelines and jump tracks from one version to another. They can occur at any time, and they help you quickly move from one level of mastery to another. Many do not realize those waves are moving through them.

There are three kinds of dimensional shifts:

+ Download dimensional shift
+ Clearing dimensional shift
+ Tsunami or earthquake dimensional shift

The **download dimensional shift** usually occurs in your dream time. The energy is stepping down while you are asleep, and you may find yourself waking up from sleep in the middle of the night. It feels like an energetic download that occurs in steps. You may wake up briefly, wonder what's going on, why you are awake, and then drift back to sleep.

It's a bit hard to describe, but you can feel this energy moving into you in stages, getting bigger and bigger, or stronger and stronger. You may feel it approach, yet it feels OK. You usually do not feel fear, and you may or may not remember it in the morning. The waking up is due to your providing some level of coherent "permission" at the physical level.

This shift causes a change in thinking without you realizing it is happening, because it allows you to change your belief system in a very, very sweet way, without working hard and without fighting with yourself for your ideas. You may go through a number of these experiences over a period of several months. It's a good thing, because it causes you to change your belief system without fighting within yourself and without having to move through it intellectually or emotionally.

The **clearing dimensional shift** is usually very subtle and gentle, and usually happens during devotional exercises or during specific aided ceremonies. It occurs by doing intense clearing work, or long meditations or ceremonies that allow your consciousness to slightly separate from identifying with the body. Sometimes the clearing work is done remotely by an expert in clearing work. Sometimes it comes from other kinds of ceremony that you may undertake with others. A clearing dimensional shift is like when you have clearing work done and you're suddenly free—and you actually feel like you have been freed. It's almost like taking a weight off your shoulders or taking off all your handcuffs.

In these cases, the reintegration of the self into the body provides for an "aha" that will level up your self-awareness and quite possibly your awareness of the world around you, along with reframing experiences of the past. You may feel like you are to be able to achieve something new, in a new or different way. You have a dramatically different feeling after you do clearing work. It can happen during a devotional exercise, so it might be your own prayer work; it might be during the process itself; it might be during a guided meditation or spiritual meditations. It can occur when you are chanting, and there may be specific ceremonies that can occur while this is happening, so these all qualify under what I call the *clearing dimensional shift*. That wave is literally allowing for timelines to merge. The energetic download is receiving the energy and ratcheting it down into you, yet it always feels like an upgrade. This may not be noticeable to you until hindsight.

The third kind of dimensional shift, the **tsunami or earthquake dimensional shift**, is a brilliant "aha" that allows you to change your belief system in one single conscious-choice moment. This kind of dimensional shift usually happens with a sudden insight. What I mean by that is, at one moment you don't think something is possible, and the next minute you are thinking, "Yes, I can do that," and you give yourself permission to do an amazing thing. As an observer, you may be working with someone or listening to someone while they are telling a story about some kind of obstacle. Then suddenly they know of or think of a way to solve it that allows them to think "I can do this!"

The shift is immediate, as the "discovery" sinks in. An outsider can observe this with an open Third Eye. It usually happens with a bit of resistance to a current situation you don't really want, yet you've not seen a way out of it, when you are more focused on the "don't want" feeling of being trapped or stuck. Suddenly, as if a jolt to your reality occurs, you literally jump tracks from your old belief system to your new one, full of possibilities. If an observer COULD see it, they would observe the room rock and sway as though you were in an earthquake or tsunami. Then, instantly, you have shifted and now are open to change, so the obstacle becomes very possible. It's also a way for you to witness someone else's dimensional shift.

Now, all dimensional shifts are literally jumping tracks. This means you are unwilling in one timeline, and are jumping to another one that is more conducive to your heart's desire, more conducive to the divine plan. This shift is permanent and allows the old version of you to fade away.

I experienced this when I was in the Akashic Records with a client and my Chinese translator in Taiwan. I built an energetic bridge with the translator, allowing her to connect with me as I receive information, to improve the translation between us. It is very effective, and she could feel my energy in real time. During this session, the client was stuck in a belief system that limited her and was actually making her emotionally miserable.

The Record Keepers told her, through me, that she did not need to accept that version of reality, and in fact, they showed her the ideal version of reality, one that was much more pleasing to her and would release her from the bondage that limiting belief held over her, which was making her life miserable. Initially she resisted, but the Record Keepers persisted, and she had that "aha" moment, allowing and considering it, and instantaneously letting go of the old view, and owning the new version.

At that moment I actually saw the room move! It literally swayed and shifted, like a wave had moved through it. At the time, I presumed it was an earthquake. After all, we were in Taiwan, and we were on the sixteenth floor! I looked at my translator, and she nodded. She had observed it also. Later, when we checked online to see what the measurement of the earthquake had been on the Richter scale, we discovered there had been no earthquake! While in the Akashic Records for myself, I asked what we had observed. The Record Keepers confirmed that it was a dimensional shift that my *client* had experienced, and both the translator and I observed as she moved from one timeline to another. You may have had similar experiences.

In 3D, we NEED linear time to sort things out, since our ability to sort out events requires limited information to navigate our experiences. The problem is, now that we are living in 5D, we have the ability to comprehend and understand more than one version of reality. In the Akashic Records, one student initially expressed confusion over this channeled message, and asked, "What limiting belief do I need to release?"

The answer came: "Time is not linear. We all move in multiple dimensions of reality whether we believe or know it. Enlightened beings are aware of this "phenomenon" but not the unenlightened ones who choose to live in darkness or refuse to see the reality because of fear of the unknown."

It is very interesting that this is directly related to multiple versions of the reality in multiple versions of you. Multiple versions of reality are based on choices you've made or regretted; multiple versions of you can be trying out various scenarios of various expression, and when this occurs you are able to tune to another version of you where were. Or maybe you're aware that you used to have a thought or a way of thinking, and that now you think differently. You may think of the multiple versions of reality as expressions of you.

You may think one is better than the other, and understand that this might come from research you were doing or ideas you have. It could be anything. It also could occur with another person, if you know one of the things a lot of people don't—that every decision entails five choices: two above grade, two below grade, and one ideal choice. That ideal choice is often counterintuitive! What happens is, just like many of the stories you've heard from me already, my Higher Self picks out a version of the future as a way to make a choice that is dramatically different from what I think I ought to do or what may seem logical. Once your Higher Self connection is clear, you will begin to see the merit of choosing to follow it. Many times, you will see that the end result also has a benefit that makes sense. For example, if you don't eat wheat or bread, but your Higher Self tells you that a pizza restaurant is the highest and best choice for you today. It makes no sense to you, since you do not eat pizza. However, when you go there, you discover that they have a wonderful salad bar, and you run into a long lost friend, and have a wonderful chat and reconnection.

MULTIPLE CHOICE

You can change the way you do things. As stated above, every decision has five possible choices: two above grade, two below grade, and one higher-self ideal choice. Your three kinds of dimensional shifts are always based on an evaluation you're going to make. Other versions of you may take the opposite choice, or they may choose based on your work with the extraterrestriasls, even if you don't know what is going on. There may be a version of you on a ship circulating around the planet, and that version needs you to move and shift, and so it occurs. In the meantime, that version of you is helping you shift and change.

A clearing dimensional shift can happen during an Akashic Records reading. It can also happen during other kinds of healing work, such as Neuro-Linguistic Programming (NLP), so understand that these are real transformational events. You are literally merging timeline versions of yourself that always thought one way, and now can be merged into one "main" lifetime.

Letting go and allowing you to move to another expression of you is very powerful. In each case, all dimensional shifts are based on a choice. Now we come back full-circle to your understanding of the dimensions that you have learned in *Waking Up in 5D*, chapter 9, which provides groundbreaking insights, allowing you to understand that you can know and experience more than one dimension and that this multidimensionality is your fundamental birthright.

··· 5 ···

Crossing Over

When you die, the seed atom in the apex of your heart is ruptured, and you detach from three of your four lower bodies: your physical body, your mental body, and your emotional body. But you retain your attachment to your desire body, which moves into your etheric (or upper) body. The etheric body can move with your intention. Your ego rises and takes the etheric (matrix) body with it, often floating above the body, usually for no more than three and a half days. The silver cord is the life-giving attachment everyone has when dreaming or having out-of-body experiences. The silver cord can stay attached for up to three days. During the three days your cord is still connected, you are doing your life review. Many of you have explored life review from reading about near-death experiences, and we will simply say it's a candid "movie" of your life, choices you've made, people you have affected and how they felt about your actions. At the time of death, the vital body (desire body) may be seen rising above the physical, deceased body.

The silver cord is still attached during your life review. It stays until the life review is complete. This is how you could be clinically dead and yet return. There are many stories of individuals going through their life review and returning to their body. A personal record exists in your DNA that allows for this. It triggers the Akashic Records, in the 11th Dimension, which then descends and autocorrects your life review where necessary.

Your desire body is attached at the liver and is connected to it in many ways. This is why you may find "entities with agendas," because they are carrying the ruminations of dissatisfaction and trying to replay them with different results in their hosts. This can also be why a deceased person's spirit may move into another family member or friend to continue the dissatisfaction, because they cannot express without an emotional body! During clearing work, they can be escorted by Archangel Michael to return home. You may think you want to keep your deceased grandma around, but the fact of the matter is that returning home is actually much better for the dearly departed, because if they need any kind of emotional or spiritual healing they can go to an etheric "hospital." A friend of mine who chose to take his life told me from spirit that he couldn't be anyone's guide "since he had many lessons to learn." The rest and rejuvenation that occur after returning home is significant.

After you have completed your life review, you then may float away from the physical body and toward something. This is where it gets tricky. Your relatives will meet you and urge you to come toward them. If you want to recycle and reincarnate, then this is probably what you will do. However, the "relatives" are really NOT relatives at all, but are holograms trying to confuse and fool you. There's a great scene in "Coda," an episode of *Star Trek: Voyager* where Janeway, the ship's captain, hovering near death, finds herself talking with her deceased father. He urges her to go with him and enter a whirling energy a few feet away. She resists and argues with him. Finally, she accuses him of NOT being her father, and pulls herself back into her body! This is a great example of what you might expect.

In another instance, a friend relayed how she and her healing partner came to work together. During a near-death experience, my friend died on a massage table—her friend and future healing partner was the masseuse! The masseuse was guided to stay with her and just wait. But then she smelled smoke and went running through her house to find the source of the fire! When she returned with no information, she was shown that her friend had been going through multiple life reviews, and "cleaning up" some of the more difficult ones. What does cleaning up mean? Looking at a difficult or horrible death with complete compassion.

At the final life review, she was burning at the stake—this is when her friend smelled smoke! A guide appeared and she was told that her life as she knew it was over. She was told that her friend, the masseuse, needed someone to work with, and she was the ideal candidate. Would she be willing to return to her body with that mission? Her response floored me!

She said to the guide, "Well, I'm not sure. I'm overweight, and have liver problems, and I have back health issues."

The Guide said they could put her soul into someone else, but there would be integration issues.

"No I don't think so," she replied.

The Guide then said, "The weight will come off over the next ten years, and we've healed your liver and back issues." Yet she STILL hesitated. I was on pins and needles waiting for the rest of this story, when she said, "Well, I was tired of not knowing what I should do next. I need to know what my next step is, if I go back."

The guide quickly responded, "Done." And she was back in her body!

Wait, I thought—she's dead, and she's negotiating? I was stunned because I thought when you die, the "free will" of choice is gone! I was wrong.

DARK NIGHT OF THE SOUL

You may have heard of the "dark night of the soul."* This phrase refers to extreme difficulty. It could be a cycle of extreme poverty or illness. You may experience a betrayal or abuse. All of these can lead to a form of despair. Your family may abandon you, or perhaps you have no one to turn to for help and comfort. The dark night of the soul is scary. It makes you think, "It's over, there is no more to life." It is the place that

---

*Described by the sixteenth-century Spanish mystic and poet St. John of the Cross in his treatise *Dark Night*, a commentary on his poem with the same name.

leads some to suicide. It's where you must rely totally on your soul's mastery, your soul's reflection on who you really are. It takes considerable effort to recover from this state. Not everyone has this experience, but most people going through this ultimately discover their own place of inner peace. It can happen proactively, where you discover your inner worth through various techniques. For example, in Vipassana,* it can occur near the end of your ten days of meditation.

The dark night of the soul phase is similar to what you will go through if you choose not to follow your relatives into the reincarnation cycle again on Earth. You must be strong and firm in your belief and conviction. You will feel all alone. You will wonder what you are doing, turning away from family and friends that urge you to join them. You will need to be clear and content with who you are, the content of your mastery, and that you and your soul know what you are doing and where you are going.

A dear soul, friend, and teacher got stuck in this vortex of recycling energy after passing unexpectedly. Many of her friends gathered to pray for her. Some of these highly connected friends could see that she was stuck in the vortex of reincarnations she didn't want. Everyone knew her desire was to continue to evolve to higher planes of existence. Yet, she couldn't seem to get out of that inevitable reincarnation vortex. Everyone wondered what to do next.

Lord Metatron stands at the edge of creation and the Void, so I suggested to the group that we ask Lord Metatron to put a tractor beam of light on her, to help her find her way through the dark night of the soul and toward Source, where she may incarnate on another planet— or Earth, as her choice. Many of her friends who could see into these realms reported she had been freed from that vortex and would be able to choose to move toward Source. Whew!

Where did she go next? This is where the understanding of the dark night of the soul is so very important. It prepares you for the dark tun-

---

*Vipassana is a popular form of meditation that involves practicing for eleven hours a day for ten days. No other form of meditation or communication is permitted, not even eye contact.

nel of choice to move toward Source. Within this tunnel, you may feel alone or abandoned. You know in your soul this is not so, but your consciousness is unfamiliar with this feeling of abandonment, unless you've prepared yourself by remembering your dark night of the soul. Using the experience of the dark night of the soul will help prepare you for this choice after passing from the Earth plane.

Some have asked the question, "Is reincarnation still going on if 3D is ending? What about the recently departed, within the past few years?"

Unfortunately, the "trap" described above will perpetuate this limited belief about polarity and 3D. The reincarnated person will need to reexperience 3D, reject it, and move into 5D. Some lessons will need to be relearned. It's so easy to go to the light of family and friends. However, choosing to return to Source will free you and pull you out of that cycle of reincarnation and the old paradigm. That's a choice you get after you die!

I had a desperate client call from a man whose mother had drowned. The man's mother was very depressed and had been rescued from drowning, but wasn't expected to live more than a day. The family wondered if it was a suicide attempt. What could be done? I immediately enlisted the help of our clearing team member Dave, who cleared her. He discovered that the mother had drowned nine times in previous lifetimes. Several drownings were punishment, a few were self-inflicted, and a few were accidents.

The family was devastated, yet, in clearing all those past lifetimes, along with outside entities and energies that didn't belong, allowed her strength to return briefly, and she lived for another nine days. This was way beyond what the doctors thought possible. This was enough time for her family to travel to her resort location, surround her with love and affection, and say their goodbyes. The man and his family were so grateful. This highlights the fact that many times we re-create circumstances we failed to resolve in the past and keep repeating them hoping for a better outcome.

Let's move to those individuals fortunate enough to go through their life review and return to tell us about it. They all discover many areas of their own belief system that were faulty. In an instant, in some cases, they can change their belief. These persons have dissolved their limiting beliefs and can now act out a new way of life. How will you discover your own beliefs that are holding you back?

You can discover patterns you may have that don't serve you. Maybe you have a tendency toward sadness, which you fall into regularly without knowing why. You cannot seem to discover the cause. It doesn't seem related to anything in the present. You just wake up one day full of sadness. This is your consciousness giving you the chance to change, by showing you what is holding you back. Maybe you've already figured out what's holding you back, but haven't sorted out how to fix it. It could be that you need entity clearing.

Maybe you can notice some of your own self-destructive patterns, which may have come from previous lifetimes. Can you fix them yourself? Your work might include not only clearing yourself of limiting beliefs but clearing at the soul level. You may try Emotional Freedom and Healing Technique, or you might try Quantum Matrix Healing. These are powerful tools for change and can often make a difference.

Emotional Freedom and Healing is a form of Emotional Freedom Technique (EFT), or tapping. Tapping is a well-known technique that utilizes Chinese meridian knowledge to direct and reframe limiting beliefs. There are many books and teachers available to support you through this, including vetted practitioners on my website.*

Quantum Matrix Healing, or QMH, is a powerful tool that uses the morphogenetic field and your Higher Self to release and repair recalcitrant behaviors you know better than to enact, but cannot seem to stop doing them—even when you want to change. This is a tool I developed that is used by practitioners who are certified to do so.

---

*StGermainMysterySchool.com.

Maximizing 5D Timelines

H ow can you create or re-create an updated version of you? Can you imagine yourself as an Ascended Master? Try including the following in your bedtime prayer: "I am my Ascended Master self, right here and now, in the physical. I am Ascended Master _____ (insert your name). I am the version of me that is already ascended." Don't put any "buts" into these phrases. Just say it to yourself at night.

HOW TIME WORKS

In 5D, all versions of time you think you know are probably out of sync with what you are capable of. You have the ability to jump timelines, and I will show you how to do that. You no longer need to "work through" issues or dramas, like the woman who drowned that I mentioned in the previous chapter. When you move into your 5th-Dimensional self, you are quite naturally in a state of unconditional love. The love itself isn't prerequisite for dimensional travel, the *purity of thought* produces the unconditional love that comes with such a shift. When you experience everything that is, everything around you, without a need to change anything at all, you are able to feel the joy of the moment, and you are then 5th-Dimensional. This creates the setup for you, and this state is *so pleasing* that you do not realize you are in the 5th Dimension. Needing to compare "where you're at" automatically drops you into 3rd Dimension, the region of polarity.

What you know about time and how time works is probably 3rd-Dimensional. The universe actually expands and contracts 264 million times per second, according to a spiritual teacher I heard this from years ago. We don't have a way to measure this, to prove or disprove, but knowing this makes so much sense! This means you are not locked into any version of how the unfolding of time will work. Imagine folding a piece of paper into a paper fan with numerous zigzag folds. Most people only look at the high points, the tops of the folds. When the fan is closed, those folds touch each other, and can represent each time the universe comes back into existence. Your experience of time is just at the top of the folded points. Knowing this, you can now move the next fold to the location in time and space you desire—you can expand and contract time! In between those folds is the gap. Deepak Chopra wrote about the gap, as did Wayne Dyer. They even offered meditations around this concept of the gap.

USING THE GAP FOR HEALING

I've used the concept of the gap for youthing exercises. I've used it to change the past and to recreate the future. Now your brain is trained and focused on returning to the last place you were, that top of the fold. I've always seen time as a series of stills. This is why you are able to create spontaneous healing. Now imagine you can slide down into the trough and choose where you come back to the top of the folds. The person who keeps announcing where they want to land, and repeats this enough, causes the summits of each fold to override the natural pattern of returning to the former sequence of the last position. This is also how the Reality Remix Meditation* works.

◆ How to Jump Timelines

Being able to jump timelines is an important tool. You may use it to help you minimize regret of something from the past and to maximize success for your future. In both cases, you are merging realities. When you change a past, you are bringing together alternate timelines that no longer work for you. As we become 5th-Dimensional, we blend multiple timelines together. Ideally your job is to be fully present in the now moment, experiencing, accepting, and integrating everything around you. When you are fully present, your reset occurs almost unnoticeably.

There are three ways to jump timelines. Take your time with this list.

1. You go to a past event and relive it, review it, then choose a more pleasing outcome. If it is an event where you regret your choices, you can use Reality Remix Meditation to help visualize a better choice for you. Many clients have reported remarkable results from this exercise, and have made significant changes quite unnoticed by them, but which produce a peace of mind not before available.

2. You can imagine a present event that has been unfolding in a difficult way, keeping awareness on one possibility—the one you do not want—then allowing yourself to see a mildly different but more pleasing outcome. Maybe you see yourself yelling at your offspring, and would like to be more gentle. The closer in time the event is to your present makes it easier to change the event in your history.

3. You can cocreate a future event by allowing the universe to show you how to develop the best "how the event occurs," without dictating the method. Instead, focus on the outcome and only the outcome. Need an extra $500? Allow your mind and heart to experience the version of the future where you already are making new choices because you already have the $500. Add a real-time conversation with someone who is "on your side," and you will amplify the energy.* This is based on the Genie principle, which shows the current situation ("you are here") along with an evolved version of the manifestation that proves the desired outcome has already occurred.

What you may not realize is that personally and collectively, humanity has the power to change the reality you know. Multiple scientific studies underscore this concept. So many times, you've been led or taught to

---

*Find detailed instructions for this in my book *Be a Genie.*

aim toward an outcome you don't want. News media is filled with stories of expected events or fearful information. What will you do with that?

You can imagine an outcome different from what you were told by news outlets or others. If you want to experiment, the first place to start is with the weather. Start thanking the weather elementals for all the good weather (even rain or snow). Before you actually move to the next step, check in with your Higher Self to ask that this proposed change in the weather will be for the highest good of all affected. Then, when something dangerous is predicted, like a tornado, you can again go to your new friends the weather elementals, asking them to soften the anticipated event or to dissolve it. When I was first told to work with the weather, I asked my Guides, "Who am I to change the weather?" They laughed and told me to research weather manipulation in China. There was a significant amount of information on the internet—from almost thirty years ago! You can imagine my surprise. Now it's your turn to ignore the mass programming and eliminate that predicted event.

The world is full of stories about humans who seem to alter time. Think of the people involved in automobile accidents who reported that everything moved in slow motion. Additionally, it has been proven scientifically that time is not absolute. As you approach the speed of light, time slows down. Research shows that astronauts have a reduction of their aging process. According to Einstein's theories of relativity, the closer you get to the speed of light, the slower time moves. In the movie *Interstellar*, they show the protagonist, played by actor Matthew McConaughey as Cooper, approaching a black hole where extreme gravity speeds up time. He moves through the black hole, passes out, is rescued, and wakes up in a hospital. The next scene is where he meets his elderly dying daughter! Remember, time is a construct. It is a group construct that you can opt out of, when you choose. Choose carefully!

You are very powerful, capable of feeling and knowing more that you think you can. When you consciously believe you are capable of interacting with time in a way that allows you to control your experience of it, you control it for everyone you are interacting with, whether they know it or not. In one example, I crossed the Sahara with my group and a police escort on a bus in three hours instead of the usual five. Upon arriving at our destination, the travel company owner, Mohamed, was waiting for us, and announced that nobody except Gregg Braden had ever done that before! I have also experienced a five-hour road trip taking only three hours!

How are these feats possible? We must move out of "scorekeeping," or keeping track. While crossing the Sahara, all of my group had fallen asleep—no time tracking there! And I was extremely focused on our destination. How will you accomplish this? Choose to avoid wearing a watch or listening to the radio with time stamps. Instead, contemplate high vibrational thoughts and focus on your destination. Use long playlists you don't know how long they are. Your focus and attention are the key ingredients. Remember, using intention and attention is also how we program the MerKaBa.* This has now been proven by science, and disclosed by Dean Radin, Ph.D.,† in talks about the studies he has done with intention in research studies in both the U.S. and Japan.

Allow yourself to focus on the outcomes you desire. Create a personal conversation in your mind's eye, and then expect the desired outcome!

We know from almost 100 years of quantum experiments that linear time is a convenient illusion that allows us to separate events and experience them separately. What is now clearly understood is that we can cross these barriers, since they are part of the construct we have subscribed to, and unhook from these barriers. This was the next step following the research on Zener cards (a deck of twenty-five cards, five of each unique symbol) to test ESP in the early twentieth century. Later research experiments were done with subjects who were exposed to random normal

---

*See my book *Beyond the Flower of Life*, p. 127.
†Dean Radin, Ph.D., chief scientist for the Institute for Noetic Sciences (IONS).

photos and then disturbing or erotic photos. The cameras filming these tests registered an actual eye movement *before* the explosive pictures were shown. These tests were just the beginning of research on time.

Experiments conducted by well-respected researcher Daryl J. Bem of Cornell University[*] over the span of about ten years involved thousands of participants and added to the data on time. Bem's discoveries demonstrated the capacity of cognition across boundaries of linear time. Dean Radin further validated these experiments and has continued to lead this new research with real science. What is totally amazing is that researcher (but layman) Mitch Horowitz[†] reports that a future exercise can improve results from the past! This is really mind bending. These experiments were conducted over the span of about ten years and involved thousands of participants. Bem's discoveries also demonstrated the capacity of cognition across boundaries of linear time.

As we dive deep into Bem's experiments in parapsychology, we discover something beyond our training of how time works! Consider that you and I have been conditioned to believe or to expect time to be linear—but it is not. Bem structured a standard cognitive test, where subjects were instructed to memorize ten words, and then tested on their retention. He conducted a series of nine experiments, with the eighth and ninth being most significant. Experiments eight and nine included a future study of the ten-word list, resulting in cognitive improvement. This demonstrated that future study had cognitive benefits in the present! Remarkable! It is just mind-boggling to think about.

After the first test, most subjects remembered five to eight words. Then a second test was given, with new words to memorize. Remember, subjects were given their memorization task and tested, but then were asked to study the same word list again, post-test. The result is astonishing—in the highly structured, rigorous second test, the scores spiked in a statistically significant way! Bem performed thousands of

---

[*]*Feeling the Future*, 2011.
[†]Institute for Noetic Sciences, *What Parapsychology Reveals "about" the Powers of Intention: A Talk by Mitch Horowitz*, recorded May 5, 2023.

these tests. His experiments in precognition demonstrated that a future event could affect the past! Even Einstein's theories support the concept of nonlinear time. Can you imagine?

This means you could study hard for an exam, take the exam, and while waiting for the results continue to study the same material, as though it could affect your score—because it does! Horowitz further tells an anecdotal story of a client who was a boxer and wanted to improve his mental sharpness. It was suggested that he complete a thirty-day thought experiment. The boxer was willing to do this—but his big match was closer than that! Mitch suggested to the boxer, based on the above-mentioned evidence, that he make a commitment to complete thirty days, regardless of the results of the match. He did that. He also won his match.

This may finally explain the Mandela effect, a theory based on the thousands of individuals who remember Nelson Mandela dying in prison, who were then shocked to learn of his release! Numerous other events have also been attributed to the Mandela effect.

In 3D, we NEED linear time to sort things out, as our ability to separate events requires information to be limited in some way in order navigate experiences. The problem is managing the multiple streams of data that are now available, as we are living in 5D. 5th Dimension is where we have the ability to comprehend and understand more than one version of reality.

When you have a busy or full life, this slowdown of activities may seem nearly impossible at times. However, I'm going to show you a number of things you can do to utilize the "bending of time" to your advantage! I watch the astrological cycles like a fisherman watches the moon phases that govern the surf. Yet, I am not an astrologer, and I don't let it rule me.

Time is malleable. Did you know? If that's so, what's with all the astrology talk? The purpose of this discussion is to expand your connection to and awareness of time and the templates that govern it. Time is thought to be mechanistic, even though we have plenty of data suggesting that time can be both compressed and expanded. This compression or expansion is solely based on our experiences—the "car accident" experience of time slowing down; the waiting forever in a customer service line.

The idea that you can control time is a new one. Most of us are so used to controlling how we use our time, we don't even realize the full potential of our power over time! Sure, it may be easier to use 3D solutions to control our world—an alarm clock instead of an inner alarm. Yet, once we learn how powerful we are and what we are capable of—it's game over for the alarm clock. Use your time wisely. Respect the things you must do, doing them first. Then imagine all the productivity being handled expertly.

WOMEN WILL LEAD

Back in 2012, I spoke about the Harmonic Convergence. I was leading a group with Gregg Braden in Chichén Itzá, when the great Mayan teacher Hunbatz Men led our group into the cave beneath the pyramid. He chose me to be the last one in and the first to lead the group out. I knew this was important. He informed us that this new era we were ushering in was to be led by women—women and the feminine energy get to lead. Will they take over or share the leadership?

The action-oriented energy (male) in each of us wants to get things done now. This is exacerbated by our current culture of instant gratification (think microwave ovens, downloadable videos, and more). Plants go through seasons, humans gestate! The path of pregnancy teaches us patience. The action of gestation is a process! A human pregnancy is started by one strong action . . . and then the waiting begins. We have historic experience of what to expect, and very little has changed over the centuries with regard to the seasons or gestation. Yet so much around us now provides some sort of gratification instantly. Let us remember that pacing has virtue. The spoiled part of us doesn't realize this is not how nature works.

Astrology gives us a little road map of what to expect. It gives us a path, an opportunity to know when to strive and when to rest and take a "time-out" from time. It gives us guidance as to when we are swimming upstream. Astrology should NOT be a dictator, but it can educate us. It can tell us what to expect humanity to do. However, it also is a movable force that we can shift and change. You can use astrology to adapt or adjust. When explaining this to a gifted astrologer friend, she commented, "I have never figured out how to move the planets." Laughing, I told her, "I don't move the planets. I move in time to a time of my choosing!" I choose to adjust time when I have a special need, and I choose to adapt to astrology when I don't have any special needs.

Like the GPS on your car or phone, when you deviate from its instructions, you are offered alternate paths. And, if you have NEVER deviated from your GPS, by the way, consider doing so! My Guides suggest that GPS came out not only as a way to help us find our way, but also as a way to get us in the habit of obeying what "the voice" says. Whoa! Doing what the voice says is a form of mind control. We usually follow our GPS precisely unless it is completely wrong! Some people often take an alternate route. It is a good practice to get in the habit of following your Higher Self rather than a computer generated voice. Take this example from a student in our annual training program. She was driving to the airport in a rental car to be dropped off before her flight. "Higher self, is it in my greatest and highest good to stop and get gas at this stop?" I would always get a "no." Even though I was getting on empty my higher self would continue to say "no." Finally closer to the airport I asked one more time and I got a "yes" answer. But what was even more profound was I got correct directions on how to get to the gas station. My higher self would say "take a right, then take a left, and one more take a right" and lo and behold the gas station was there. It was also a snacks shop, so I got my snacks, and the gas was way cheaper than any place on the way to the airport. This is my favorite story, and I use connection to my higher self on everything, every day. I also think it's very important that we use the correct wording when connecting to our higher self to get the proper responses.

Remember, astrology is a template. It is part of the 3D game set up for humanity's highest and best good. Humans are gradually shifting out of time as a *mechanistic experience* to a more fluid expression, and learning to experience time as event-based, instead of mechanistic. This is a move from the Divine Masculine way to the Divine Feminine way. Part of this is to move through the time/space continuum with flow and ease, becoming 5th-Dimensional.

Because Astrology is a template, it's like the "setup" for a game of chess or a video game. All the "men" on the board have certain possible moves, along with limitations of what they may and may not do. It's up to the player to utilize these moves to their advantage. Learning any strategy game is useful because it creates in you the ability to imagine possibilities. The game of chess is one such game. If you've never learned to play chess, it is worth the effort. Or take an easy way, and buy an app that stimulates your mind. This is important, so you don't get stuck in a form of thinking that reinforces the vibe being beamed at you via airwaves, cell phone towers, and Wi-Fi. Mentally challenging games stimulate your discriminating thinking, which is very necessary during these unpredictable times.

The metaphor of astrology being a template is important because it helps you see that you have the advantage—if you will use it! How will you use your "thinking" advantage? First, recognize that this template is part of the "setup" for the game of life. Being aware of the trends and movement of society as a whole doesn't predict them, but it does provide a strong indicator. That's why marketers, stock market traders, and presidents have used astrology to ensure their success.

I use a simple prayer to align myself with the energies of astrology, and then "step out of them" periodically, as needed, for special assignments or special events. It's important to realize how allowing the template of astrology to guide our actions, because it sets the stage for rest, allows for renewal and growth. You get to choose how to recognize when you need to step outside of one template of astrology that governs humans. Governing humans is one way to put the game in motion. Your free will has sovereignty over the template. But, just like your GPS will tell you when there is a traffic slowdown, you must manually choose a different route to avoid it. The Antidote for Mercury Retrograde is like that (see appendix 2).

Next, work on your sovereignty. This is a little more challenging, since most people do not realize how much power they have given away, or how much they have. Your power gets taken away in many ways, but always because we may unknowingly allow it. This occurs when we mindlessly turn on certain programming, internet or TV shows, to unwind from a long or stressful day. Sometimes this takes the form of advertising or marketing to you; other times it is an addiction to a show or "Thursday night" special shows.

One powerful tool to help you stay in your power when around powerful people who can sometimes run roughshod over you is the Orion pendant from Vibranz.* It helps you hold your ground, yet be completely loving and supportive. I believe almost half the population has some form of narcissism. You can tell a narcissist because they will tell you what to do instead of sharing what they have experienced. They will "solve" your problems before you have asked them to . . . instead of listening. Finally, the biggest narcissists have trouble with compromise, and need to feel that their ideas and suggestions are the best ones. One therapist I've worked with extensively, who has also worked for judges and big corporations, considers narcissism as a major issue among high-level managers. She says that the hardest-working people are narcissistic, and are the most difficult to fire because they get so much done. Dealing with this is another discussion. It is important to find ways to stay in your power.

Your sovereignty allows you to instinctively know what you need to know or do, when you need to know or do it. Each and every one of us—all of humanity—is increasing their abilities to tune in and know their best course of action! You can get hijacked by energies that will give you good information and then alternate it with troubling information.

Conclusion: The time experiment results were repeated thousands of times, and replicated by countless researchers, challenging our belief in

---

*PureVibranz.com/maureenst.

the static nature of time. Future study improved the results of the test. Remember, time is a construct that humanity has adopted and adapted to. We have collectively subscribed to it. But you can opt out! You can change how you adapt and choose to opt out of time, specifically in order to achieve something. I don't recommend you opt out permanently, because you might become mentally unstable. Some of your experiences may include intergalactic influence that can transcend linear time. These outside influences can be part of prehistory and can be dropped into the time/space continuum, changing reality for a few or many.

THE LORDS OF TIME ARE TEACHING US ABOUT MERGING TIMELINES

You may have heard that time is nonlinear. But what does that really mean? In my books and classes, I've referred to time as a construct—some would say a necessary construct. I say time is a *mutable* construct that we are learning to manipulate.

I have repeatedly manipulated time during a Mercury Retrograde by using a simple prayer that I teach in the Akashic Records (see appendix 2). I've arrived an hour early two different times when flying on United Airlines from Detroit, where I used to live, to a city in Hawaii, where the departure time was an hour after the scheduled takeoff! Both examples started with a delayed flight, one in Hawaii, one in Detroit. You can read more about that in *Opening the Akashic Records*.

In yet another example, I interviewed a candidate for the Ascension Institute, who later joined our program. In our interview, I invited her to ask me any question for which she might desire another opinion. She was quick to come up with a burning question she'd had since childhood. She reported that many times as a child she would become "frozen," unable to move, but she could "see" time, with things in the future going really fast, and at other times time seeming to be in slow motion. This is like those times when your internet connection on a Zoom meeting is "iffy," and the person on the other end is "frozen," but then they suddenly move very fast. She has had this experience as recently as a few years ago! Even though she has asked many experts, no one has ever been able to give her an explanation that made any sense to her.

I explained that I felt this was a dimensional shift she was experiencing, and that dimensional shifts cause one to jump timelines. Not many observe, or are even aware of, these dimensional shifts. I showed her my PowerPoint presentation on this subject, so she could see I wasn't making this up on the fly. I then went on to explain to her my communications with the Lords of Time. She asked, "Have you ever seen anything from anyone else about the Lords of Time?" I told her no, and that they had come in with such force in their very first communication with me that their presence was unmistakable the initial time they channeled through me. While I'm explaining this to her, the Lords of Time tell me she is one of them! Immediately I get body confirmation in a really big way, and so does she—with confirming goose bumps all over her body. This description felt like a match.

The following Sunday, I'm on a FaceTime call with my husband while in China, and get an interrupting call from my book agent. When I ask why she is calling (it's Saturday for her) she says, "You called me!" I report that I had not and had been on the phone with my husband for the past fifteen minutes. Within a few minutes another call comes in, this one from my former husband, who I am on good terms with. He explains that I accidentally deposited a large sum of money into his account! I asked him how he knew it was my money, and he said it was from my book agent (for royalties from my book sales). I said that's really strange, but maybe it went into our former joint account, which he had taken over. No, he said it went into his business account! How was this possible? She didn't have his banking data, nor did I! Just the night before, I was telling my husband about the time-related experiments and how researchers were performing experiments that proved precognition, challenging the notion that time was linear. How was this possible?

Both calls came in unsolicited while I was on the phone with my husband. Yet each of them was related to an incorrect bank deposit that had come up at that time, as if I had called them! For years I've referred to time, saying, "There is plenty of time to do everything that is important to me, and I have everything I need before I need it." I think the Lords of Time have more to say.

The following day, I received a call from my assistant. I'd sent her an email on Saturday saying I would not be calling her as planned, as I'd realized the requested call was on a Saturday, and I didn't want to disturb her weekend. I asked if it would be OK to phone her at 4 p.m., her time, on Sunday, since that would be Monday for me. She never got that email, I discovered, because she has messages silenced on Saturday. Yet, like clockwork she called me at the appointed time! She, like the others, said, "You just called me." I had been on the phone with my husband for the preceding twenty minutes!

Finally, I asked the Lords of Time what was going on. Was this confusion meant to somehow fill in information from the future event of discovering the bank error? Was there more understanding of what had been transpiring?

THE LORDS OF TIME
CHANNELED THROUGH MAUREEN J. ST. GERMAIN
Hong Kong, August 6, 2023

These are the Lords of Time, who are here to answer your questions. As you have surmised, what is happening is you are observing adjacent timelines that are showing up to show you that one timeline is slightly ahead of the next the one. What you are experiencing in your present is out of calibration with another version of you that is slightly ahead of this. Your abilities to inhabit your own timeline ahead of time is what is allowing this to occur. This means that you are capable of participating in more than one timeline.

This also means that it is another opportunity for you to demonstrate multidimensionality with your readers, who will begin to understand that they too may have experiences like this where a version of themselves is already taking action on something that they plan on doing, but have not yet done.

Now, for your participants and for your readers, we want you to imagine the times that you wake up just before your alarm goes off. Or, similarly, you finish your one-hour meditation before your timer goes off.

You come out of it, you wonder why you are finished ahead of time, and then the timer announces that the allotted time has gone by. What this means is that a version of you is complete. Even though you may have jumped to the conclusion, "Oh I could've slept for five more minutes" or "Oh, I could've meditated for a few more minutes," the fact remains that another version of you has already completed the task you were on. This means you may jump to this new timeline and accept the fact that you are already complete. This will improve your ability to fast-track into anything that you wish to work on.

Now there are studies, as you are writing, about where a person can know something a few seconds into the future. Researchers have taken photographs, as you know, and proved that the subject's eyes would recognize a disturbing picture before it was actually shown. Further studies have also demonstrated that humans can study **after** a test to improve the results.

What we want you to understand is, when you make a commitment to yourself to meditate every day for a month or two, to run every day for the next month, or to sit down and write every day at a certain time, you are actually changing the present moment because those future actions will improve the situation that you are in. Your ability to tap into the version of you that has completed the writing assignment or that has completed the weight loss or has completed the cycle that you promised yourself produces an improved outcome in the present. This is why your commitments and your determination produce your destiny. This is because all parts of your experience are going on simultaneously.

From a linear vantage point, it looks like you are dipping into the future to progress the past or to improve the present. We say it's all happening simultaneously, so when you are a person who keeps their commitment consistently, who is working on self-improvement constantly, you will gain a huge boost in your outcomes and the results that you achieve will be substantial.

This is also why the message from your beloved El Morya stands so strongly in your consciousness. His message, which basically states "I don't care if you fall down, I just want to know you're going to get up," is so important. It says to yourself, as a human, that you can re-create your present by the efforts that you have made in the future because you know you're going to do it.

We offer our deep love and appreciation for this channel and her willingness to bring forward our educational training. She has received this training three times before she began to finally understand that she was literally viewing more than one timeline, and that she can merge them and keep going at a much faster pace.

We also want you to imagine, if you will, that you are in a video game where you have more than one version of you in the game, you have many players and, like a racing event where the baton is passed from runner to runner, you are racing your car at full speed and another version of you passes you. At which point, you jump into that car and that car goes along the faster timeline, and yet another version of you comes along, passes you, and you jump into the next timeline that allows you to fast-forward, to fast-track into the highest outcome you can possibly produce. This is substantial.

THE LORDS OF TIME
CHANNELED THROUGH MAUREEN J. ST. GERMAIN
October 26, 2021

We are the Lords of Time, and we wish you to understand that there are timelines that are merging and coalescing for your Highest Good. Many of you are aware of experiences that don't seem to add up, experiences that can be perceived as a strange dream. But we ask you to hold in your heart the most evolved version for humanity possible.

You don't know what that is, all the time, but you do know it might not be what you're experiencing. The way around this is to simply notice that everyone is happy, everyone is joyful, everyone is working things out. Much can be said for all of the information you find on the internet, but it is most important that you develop your own connection so that you can validate what you experience for yourself.

Some versions of time are almost what you might call "a done deal." However, the more you visualize that things work out, that things that you have observed in reality, no matter what you are observing, are giving an outcome that pleases people, you are helping it happen easier and sooner. Maureen calls it "belief, in the absence of evidence."

If you're tired of whatever it is that's going on in your life and you want to see some change, do those meditations. Or just take a moment and imagine that you're in a place or time of the future, where it all worked out and everybody is breathing easier and things are amazing and people are astonished. We ask you to prepare to be amazed.

We also say there may be some darkness that you will you encounter—difficult people, crazy situations, scary moments. We remind you that this part of the reality is only to slow you down—and when you recognize that, you can step out of it. Remember that fear and worry are perversions of time. Fear is a perversion of the past because you fear what you know or what you've heard of. Worry is fear that something similar could happen. Neither serve you—and they are misuses of time. Fear or worry are good once—to cause you to shift and change, to decide "I'd better take care of that."

We've all had those moments where you were given a message—"take care of this," "do that"—and you ignored it and then discovered you "coulda, shoulda"—because something happened. So, pay attention to those messages and act on them in a timely fashion. And if you're worried you don't have enough time to get everything done, we will offer you this simple prayer: "I am asking for everything that I need to accomplish to be done on time and in plenty of time."

We further ask you to think of time like a ribbon—and that ribbon can be stretched or pushed together, it can be looped to produce outcomes that happen simultaneously. This will be the discussion of another lesson that Maureen will give at some point in the future [see above message]. Your understanding of time is a gift to enjoy each and every moment. It allows you to segregate experiences. Memory allows you to reexperience time. When you allow your memories to rule, once again, you have taken time out of context. Ask us to teach you about time. You'll be amazed at the information you'll come up with. And Maureen is wanting you to make sure you tell her if you get some fabulous piece of information (laughs). You are all blessed. You are all safe. The best time is yet to come—and we will close with that.

· · · 7 · · ·

Arriving in 5D
with Family and Friends

The new frequencies are significantly different from our 3D reality. So much so, that it would cause cognitive dissonance or some kind of emotional reaction (perhaps unpleasant) for you if you could access them before you are ready. This is why you may resist or why family members may resist. Even when you yearn for family members to join you in your thinking, their own belief systems may be so entrenched that releasing their version of reality would cause them significant inner discord.

Let's put this into perspective. How many people do you know who are continuously improving themselves? How many people are proactively working toward a better and better self? If this is you, bravo! Maybe your family members are content with themselves, or too entrenched in their habits, or just too lazy to shift. Sometimes the change doesn't occur until they face some significant aha moment. Then you can be there for them, to help them reorient themselves in a new plane of existence.

As we learned in the last chapter, committing to any program of improvement, exercise, meditation, eating choices, etc., will be greatly magnified—not just a little, but significantly—by our commitment to following through—and then actually following through. You have a mission here on Earth. You may attempt to be someone who is here to help others, to make a difference. Your willingness to work at this with dedication will take you where you want to go. Yet, sometimes humans fail. Sometimes you ruminate about those failures. What I learned many years ago through my study of spiritual teachings is that failure isn't the problem; the problem is whether we recover again or not! At one point in my life, I had a house, three children at home, a debt load bigger than I had income for, no savings, and had just gotten fired from my job. I was terrified. I remember wailing to myself, "What will I do?" over and over, like a pain-filled mantra, when the voice of the Ascended Master El Morya (whose focus is the will of God) announced in my head, "JUST SHOW UP." For sure, I stopped wailing and wondered, "What does that mean?"

What does it mean to you, to show up? Not everyone shows up. Can you? Can you take one step into your mastery by choosing to show up? I decided El Morya's message meant that I had to get serious about job hunting and serious about growing my budding seminar business. I converted a space in my home to a proper office, and showed up every day to work from 8 a.m. to 5 p.m. I gave myself one hour for lunch, and worked on my job search and growing the seminar business every day until things picked up and a new job was offered. I had a lovely garden where I loved to spend time, but recognized that my "work" wasn't there. I loved to cook, but again, cooking was reserved for before or after work. And forget about my wonderful hobby of sewing my own clothes! I was now on a mission!

Now, it's important to understand that the daily practice itself will contain challenges. Just like New Year's resolutions that slip by the wayside in mid-February—you need a plan for when that happens. So, no matter how many days have gone by where you've missed your daily practice, determine before you go to bed that "I am getting up in time to do my meditations." *Atomic Time*, a multi-million-dollar bestseller written by James Clear, provides a brilliant path to creating and releasing habits. It is an incredible resource to help you stay focused, learn about your own behavior, and improve your outcomes.

One of my strategies is to have shortcuts for those times I am ready and willing to do my meditation practice, but just don't have enough time. This energy is different from the forgetting behavior, where you simply forgot to fit it in. This means you know the work you must do, and you shorten it in some way to accomplish the same thing. For example, there is a ten-minute morning prayer in the book *Reweaving the Fabric of Your Reality*, but there is a much shorter prayer (one minute) in the front of the book that I have included here. Use it when you are really pressed for time.

Morning Prayer

I ask that the full expression of my highest self be ever present with me this day. I ask for the Masters, Teachers, and Guides of me to be ever present this day and ask that they be given full access to my four lower bodies.

I offer myself in humble gratitude in service to the Great White Brotherhood, legions of 100 percent White Light and all beings of 100 percent White Light who are here working with me.

I ask that this divine guidance assist me and allow me to pursue my soul's highest purpose in this lifetime with the most evolved appearance possible that expresses in the kindest, most generous, and gentle way. Amen.

Finally, understand the content of the prayers you do. For example, the morning prayer is your commitment to be in alignment with your Higher Self and to Source. If you don't have time for the short prayer, then say this:

Dear Source, I'm committed to being my best self today, and I'm asking my Higher Self to help me accomplish this.

I discovered by accident that prayers have the greatest impact when read, rather than memorized, and spoken out loud. Initially, I was saying my

Bedtime Prayer silently as I read it. Then one day, I invited my husband to say it after me, in a call and response. We began taking turns saying it out loud in phrases for the other to repeat. It is this hearing and saying that fully activates your mind and body to produce the most effective results.

TOOLS FOR NAVIGATING DIFFICULTIES

When you have interactions with people, ask your Higher Self and your dragons to handle the details. This is especially important when you have meetings and discussions scheduled ahead of time. Always ask your Higher Self to negotiate for you. Why should you include your dragons? Dragons are all about clarity and will help you to be succinct in getting your points across easily.

Call In Your Dragons Meditation

I am asking for my dragons of light to show up! I am asking them to make themselves known to me and to help me in all areas they excel in, such as clarity! I am grateful for their presence in my life.

A key takeaway from the Call In Your Dragons Meditation: Your dragons are real. When you call to them, they are very responsive. I've had many testimonials from readers of my book *Waking Up in 5D*, who wrote sharing their surprise and delight at meeting the dragons and enlisting their help.

One member of my yearlong program the Ascension Institute wrote to me recently regarding a discussion we'd had at our last retreat, about how to ask our Higher Self and the dragons to intercede and negotiate for us in the dream time. He wrote:

"I was in a quasi-battle with my former employer about my final pay. I asked my Higher Self and my dragons to negotiate for me ahead of our next meeting, in the dream time. I am just finished our last meeting with great success! I had been negotiating with them for months, and just a few days after asking my Higher Self and dragons for assistance, I got the settlement I wanted!"

If you are familiar with my work on the MerKaBa, you may have heard me say that you can be 5D by wearing the MerKaBa—without having earned it. This is timeline jumping! You learned about this in chapter 6. It takes so little to announce "I'm waking up in 5D" just before falling asleep. I keep a copy of the complete Bedtime Prayer in my suitcase and in my bedside table.* Even though I have it memorized, I find it is so much more powerful when I read it out loud, because it engages both my mind and my voice. It's an act of will, too, because sometimes I am too tired to read it, but do anyway. You can too! This quasi-awake/quasi-asleep time, the transitional state from wakefulness to sleep, is called hypnagogia. *Hypnagogia* is also defined as "the waning state of consciousness during the onset of sleep." Its opposite, the transitional state from sleep into wakefulness, is called *hypnopompia*. Mental phenomena that may occur during these "threshold consciousness" phases include hypnagogic hallucinations, lucid dreaming, and sleep paralysis.† These states of mind have been proven to be incredibly powerful for auto-suggestion, which we will discuss in this chapter.

The Bedtime Prayer is probably one of the most important tools I use. I can tell when I've forgotten, or when I've just been too tired to say it. Even if you can recite it from memory in bed, it is still preferable to read it, so you are fully engaged. If you fall asleep saying it, your Higher Self may finish it for you. I have included this wonderful tool in appendix 1.

When you are in a real-time challenging discussion with someone who is important to you, you can ask for a time-out. You can say, "I'm not up for this right now. Could we continue this at a later time?" Be willing to specify that later time. And then reach for your resources, including the dragons. Ask the dragons and your Higher Self to handle the resolution in the dream time. Prepare to be amazed.

When you have snapped or yelled at someone (usually because of the presence of entities—yours or theirs), and they quickly apologize or

*An updated version of the Bedtime Prayer is found in appendix 1.
†Wikipedia, "Hypnagogia."

perhaps look or act hurt, you can let them know you regret overreacting. Sometimes we don't know the power of our influence over others, and our harsh reactions need to be diffused before too much time goes by.

Keep a gratitude list. I fold an 8.5 x 11" paper in half, the long way. At the top of the left-hand column, write "To Do," on the right, "Gratitude." Make sure to write the names of the people and situations in your life you are grateful for. I learned from Feng Shui expert Peg Donahue that each of us generally can do about seven projects daily. So even when I make a big list of everything on my mind, I then prioritize the highest ones, with the help of my business manager, and hand off the things that others can do for me. As my business manager pointed out recently, most of us do all the little, easy things first—which may eat up all the available time needed for the important things.

Keep a journal. Keep your notes handy, so you can review your ideas and classes you've signed up for and attended. Use the same notebook for everything (unless you have a "Bring in Your Beloved" special journal of love letters).

I would like to invite you to work with Ascended Master Amen Bey, who can provide assistance to help you heal your four lower bodies, and cleanse and clear your three-fold flame in your heart. He will direct needle-point rays (pink for Love, yellow for Wisdom, and blue for Power) into every cell and atom of your four lower bodies, allowing for the channeling of miracles. Ascended Master Amen Bey has had many Egyptian lifetimes, and served as a pharaoh in Egypt. He can teach you, if you request his tutoring on cosmic law. Just think, you can develop a relationship with him, which will help the inner you to be prepared for ascension. Remember, every human who puts himself into this can achieve results faster! If you see a deep blue hieroglyph in your mind's eye, you are working with him on inner planes.

This era of transition to a 5th-Dimensional reality moves upon us whether we are ready or not. You may default to your old behaviors, thoughts, patterns, and habits in the new paradigm, where they no longer "fit." The opportunity to listen to our friends and family when they call us out is offered. What shall we do? Perpetuate the excuse or explanation? Or shall we look at these observations as an opening to shift and change? What will you do when you have worked hard to make yourself an authority to others perhaps because you want to be helpful to others or because you actually think you are right? Maybe it's time to take off the "mom" hat, or the "expert on everything" hat!

Maybe self-improvement sounds daunting? What about making fewer mistakes? A military man told me that, when he's working, he's not finished until he's checked everything two times, per military protocol. How many times do you double-check your work? Lou Gehrig's manager said Gehrig never made the same mistake twice. What can we learn from the Japanese art of *Kaizen*, or continuous improvement? There is even a mathematical theory that states that looking back to see how or what you did, and then choosing to improve it a little bit (even 1 percent) will improve you thirty-seven times more than if you did nothing. Like compounding interest, if you give yourself the gift of paying attention to every day, choosing in the moment to improve just a bit, you are going to improve! How many times did you meditate last week? How can you open your third eye? How do you activate the pineal? Every meditation you give yourself comes from your desire for continual improvement. You can even use meditations aimed at solving a problem or improving a situation.

There is a common phrase lots of people know: "I'm getting better and better every day." Not too many know it was popularized by a man who was a pharmacist by day and a mind theorist by night. Without the benefit of modern research, 100 years ago Coué theorized that if you said, "Day by day I am getting better and better" twenty times right before sleep (during hypnagogia) and twenty times right upon awakening (during hypnopompia), it would have a significant impact on your life.

"It is always the imagination that wins over the will, without exception."

"I'm getting better and better every day."

ÉMILE COUÉ, *SIMPLE SELF-HEALING*

What does all this have to do with your family? When they observe your happiness, caused by looking at yesterday and doing one thing a little better today, it will inspire them. If it does not, no matter, you can still include them in your prayers and manifestations, such as the Golden Time Meditation.* You won't need to tell them much, and it's preferable if you do not, so you don't scare them off. Share one little thing when they ask, and then change the subject. It will help them to feel safe. They have opened their mind. Wait till they ask more questions. This is when their curiosity has turned into admiration, and they truly want to know more. Their heart and head are now engaged. This is when you make a difference, by inspiring them.

This change in the world that you hope for, that we all hope for, is coming, albeit slowly. Everyone will have the chance to be an Ascended Master on the Earth, living, loving, sharing, growing, and evolving. The best way to lead is not by persuasion, but with patience and by example.

Over the course of six or twelve months, could you envision yourself becoming this Master? What will you choose? It doesn't take a lot of experience to become a Master, you just bring in what you need. The problem is, most people reading this book already have mastery in them, but are you learning anything in between where you are today and your arrival as a Master? Many people live life, and do not improve. Those that would have you fail, would want to lull you into inertia. How do you break out of inertia? What if you used the bedtime phrase, "Every day, I'm expressing as the Ascended Master me." This small phrase will help wake up dormant gifts you've yet to embrace and express. Using the Crystal Elohim Meditation,* specifically track 13, the Turquoise Elohim, will give you insight as to how to make this request and how to personalize it for you.

Crystal Elohim Meditation
Elohim! I am asking for help with living my
5th-dimensional life.

A key takeaway from the Crystal Elohim Meditation: The Elohim can give a boost to your everyday activity. Because they are the builders of form, they are ideally suited to help you create the life you desire. In this meditation, they are coupled with crystal rays to help you experience them in a very specific way. A client of mine, happily married for twenty-five years, experienced the most challenging week of his life when his business slumped, he felt unwell throughout the week, and his wife asked for a divorce! At the end of that week, he was scheduled to meet with his men's group to do a mountain climb. Chanting "Elohim" with each exhale, despite being late and the last to begin the climb, he managed to be the first to reach the top. You can grasp the significance of this triumph!

✳

As we learned in the last chapter, pay attention to the random pocket calls, surprise calls or music on your device, and other ticklers your Angels and Guides give you! The messages may actually be from a future you!

ARE YOU CONNECTING WITH OTHERS?

I was on a flight to Los Angeles, after the pandemic was coming to a close and everyone was still wearing masks. The plane was surprisingly noisy, like a bar or a tin-roofed restaurant. I listened to the conversations of people around me. One man was sharing his exploits as a scuba diver and surfer (the more you surf, the poorer you get, he said). His seatmate revealed that she had nine children.

Across the aisle and behind me was another woman, on her fourth flight that day, trying to get somewhere amid canceled or changed flights. I was amazed at the detail I was hearing! I wondered to myself if I suddenly had Wonder Woman hearing! Meditating on this, I asked what was going on. Connection!

All these passengers, having been isolated for years, were subconsciously seeking connection with strangers in a big way. It seemed like each one was talking to someone, or multiple people, not just their travel mates, but strangers. I found it quite endearing.

What is it about connection that compels us to reach out to strangers, even while wearing a mask? I think part of it was that the fear had dissipated from so many who were closed down due to all kinds of fear issues being projected on humans. It seemed that people were ready to share their experiences. Remember, much of the fear projected onto humans did not originate in actual facts.

This feeling of wanting to belong falls right in with Maslow's third and fourth hierarchy of needs: love and belonging, and esteem. The telling of stories to a willing listener takes us into self-actualization. It's so much easier to self-actualize as you tell your story to another interested human while they express sincere interest and compassion.

Sometimes, though, we have residue of unresolved feelings—disappointments that didn't deliver our heart's desire. What if you are still carrying some "rejection" baggage? This may limit your ability to connect (or heal) at the deepest levels. Perhaps you have created filters of negativity or bitterness that cannot be dissolved by traditional methods of healing traumas caused by events such as that long-lost love that didn't work out, creating a space for that special someone, or the one that "got away." The feeling of being left behind can occur even if you were the person who broke away. There are many powerful resources to help you resolve past baggage. Many of them do not require that you "process" step by step, in the old ways.

Resources for Self-Improvement

Higher Self connection	Tapping
Clearing work	Matrix Energetics
QMH (Quantum Matrix Healing)	Guided Meditations (Illuminate app)
Akashic Records Training or readings	Essential Oil Blends: Orion Series
Feng Shui	Special Pendants

A CLEARING MANTRA

While in Los Angeles, I ran into a lovely friend and her new sweetheart. She had been in Egypt with me just six months earlier and had become a good text friend. I was eager to hear her news, because our correspondence had revealed that, the day after returning from our Egypt trip, her boyfriend (who had been planning to move in with her) dumped her, over the phone! Can you imagine coming home to that? As if that weren't enough disappointment, she'd also been expecting a big promotion, which she had interviewed for, with the company she'd been with for three years. Upon her return from her fantastic Egypt vacation, she learned she was passed over for the promotion she'd been promised!

The universe has an amazing way to help us heal. She had practiced a very special mantra in every temple we'd visited. The day following her discovery that she didn't get the promotion, she received an offer from another company, a competitor—and it was a much better offer!

Her old company promised to make a counter offer, which took a few days, however it wasn't very special, so she turned it down. A day later, a third company's CEO called her with a fabulous offer that she didn't even interview for! She accepted it. A week later, she met her now boyfriend, who she started dating a few months later. She was eager to tell me about her secret—which she had practiced during our trip to Egypt.

As a group, when we went into each temple in Egypt, I instructed each participant to make a clear intention about what they wanted, explaining the purpose of each of the initiations we would be taking in each temple. In her case, she asked for the same thing at every single temple. What did she ask for?

Remember, she hadn't been unhappy at all—she had a good job, a promotion in sight, and a boyfriend who was moving in with her and toward commitment. She asked for "Love and friendship at the deepest level." And now you can too! Special update: They are now engaged, and by the time you read this will be married!

Let's clear out anything that is standing in the way of your ideal life, anything that may stand in the way of your true happiness, and claim love and friendship at the deepest level. Now and forever. If you think you might benefit from clearing out whatever doesn't serve you, this is the mantra for you! It will either strengthen what you have or dissolve it. The waiting is over. Whenever you feel dissatisfaction about anything in your life, say: "I ask for love and friendship at the deepest level." Watch the old unserving parts of your life dissolve while the ideal, magical life begins.

Resurrection
and Ascension

Resurrection and *ascension* are two terms that have a lot of 3D con-
notations to them. Both imply a death of some sort, while implying new life and regeneration. Unfortunately, these terms are a little
outdated because they fail to help you understand that you are literally
morphing into a new being, most unlike what you have been. Think of
the butterfly's path from insect (worm) to beautiful creature. We call
this the chrysalis stage. They don't die between those stages—at some
point they completely liquefy inside the pupa! You won't have to liquefy
to become the Ascended Master You, don't worry.

The true nature of what is happening to humanity is a form of the
chrysalis stage. If we can accept this concept about ourselves, we can
move forward with grace and ease. As we become 5th-Dimensional,
many changes are taking place in the human body, the four lower bodies, and the consciousness. In chapter 6, I reminded you that you can be
in 5D without having earned it, by wearing the MerKaBa. Your activating this field is the basis for the 8D MerKaBa, which will be discussed
later in this book.

Let's start with the human form and go from there. You have four
lower bodies. Each of them must align with your higher consciousness
and be the evolved version of itself. How you handle your energy is
more important than achieving physical perfection. Growing the physi-

cal energy is best expressed through activating chi. The best way to do that is through the original martial art, Qi Gong, which elevates and activates the chi you breathe into tangible energy to improve stamina and general health.

Mother Earth has four lower bodies as well. The spiritual plane is the place where creation was started by the founders. Each level below it is more dense. According to Jaap van Etten, each of the four bodies is inhabited by you and contains multiple levels. Connecting to your Oversoul (Celestial Soul) allows you to channel healing, abundance, and transformation, as described in earlier chapters.

The four lower bodies are light vehicles that have consciousness and are directly related to your consciousness. They do not lead, but reflect the experiences you take in. Therefore, they are receptors and warehouses for information collected from human experiences. They are collecting data from the five senses, along with the seven chakras. If your Higher Self is connected and used regularly, it is also contributing to the data expansion. Know that all that data is orgasmic to Source—it is so pleasing and expansive, it contributes to Source's delight. Your every experience is your raison d'être (the most important purpose for being). Be in gratitude that you are the resource for this expansion.

THE PHYSICAL BODY

Your presence here on Earth depends upon your being in a body. Therefore, you owe it to your body to take good care of it. Other parts of you depend on you doing your part in the physical. In terms of the four lower bodies, your physical body is the most important element, even though each of us wants balance between all four lower bodies. It's funny when you think about this, but you could be walking around with pains in your emotional or etheric body, or even your mental body, but when you suffer from pain in the physical body you very likely will stop everything to fix it. Consider taking this step for healing the other three bodies as well.

Your physical body is the conduit through which you receive and convey your experiences of the world. Your presence here is extremely important. As part of the recognizance team here on Earth, you may be surprised to learn that your presence on the Earth may be a function of bringing more light to the planet! Being present in your body is sometimes difficult when you've had emotional trauma. Whether you are fully human or a hybrid, your physical presence is paramount.

Your physical body is the experiencer of consciousness. Without a body, you are only consciousness. When you lose your physical body, as in death, you lose your emotional body and mental body as well. The etheric body can move and replicate a feeling of having a physical body to the etheric senses, but not to other people. When you died, your etheric body could also move into someone else's body, as a ghost. We call that spirit possession.

If you are reading this, you have a physical body. If you have a physical body, you also have a body elemental. Your body elemental is a gift from Mother Earth. She bestowed this body elemental in you to help you acclimate to this Earth. In a study intended to learn the natural rhythm of the human, performed in Las Vegas at a place without windows, subjects were allowed to do whatever they wanted with their time, including play games, read, sleep, etc., but not any timed events, like movies or music. What the study found is that the average cycle for humans is twenty hours awake, ten hours sleeping. When I learned this, I realized that humans couldn't be from here! This is one more reminder of how very important the body elemental is for helping us fit in here on Earth.

Physical, mental, emotional, and spiritual violence of all kinds leave an energetic imprint until cleared. So, you may want to begin to understand the power you hold in each of your four lower bodies, and how to maximize that to minimize trauma.

If your body is a spaceship—and it is—and you name it the *Enterprise*, then your body elemental would be "Scotty." It helps to have a perspective on what exactly the body elemental does. It runs all your autonomic processes and keeps your body running smoothly. You can train your body and body elemental to respond to your commands with autogenic training. There is a lot of scientific evidence to prove you can train your autonomic muscles, the lungs and stomach, along with other organs. The Mind Mastery for 5D Meditation* helps with this self-training. It is based on the simple principles of autogenics.

As a healing technique, autogenics has been around for over eighty years. Autogenics is a modality, a self-regulating technique that teaches your body to respond to your commands, so you can gain control of your heart rate, digestion, breathing, and more! Although it is not completely understood how it works, it is scientifically proven to help individuals with chronic stressful conditions such as asthma to train the body to avoid dropping into a crisis modality. I recorded a guided autogenic meditation for myself, and then made it available to the public. I added binaural beats to enhance the efficacy of the training.

I've used it several times when I had severe allergic reactions to mold or other airborne substances while dealing with lung problems. You may give your body elemental continuing education for a variety of skills that you may need, health issues that need to heal, and also instructions so you can stay youthful. You can instruct your Higher Self to escort your body elemental to schools in the etheric in order to learn new skills and to acquire the latest technology for rapidly emerging crystalline-based bodies. Never send your body elemental for continuing education on its own. It doesn't have a will, and relies on programming—your Higher Self must be the escort. You may also activate the self-healing DNA cells that were disengaged from your original divine DNA blueprint. I knew our self-healing DNA had been shut down, and I also knew they were the key to long life and restoration and healing.

I meditated for a year trying to figure this out, once I knew there were beings that had disconnected this self-healing DNA, which is the part of you that also regulates aging. Concerning our missing DNA strands, the fallen Angels could not steal them, even though they managed to disconnect and hide them. I finally realized they had tucked them into a lower dimension, where we would not be likely to look as we ascended.

Your body will give you messages when you train yourself for this. Have you ever had that sinking feeling when you know bad news is coming, or the feeling of joy or anticipation when you know good news is on the way? Maybe your heart has "skipped a beat" when you meet someone or you connect with a long-lost friend. Higher Self connection training relies on recognizing the body sensations that come in as "yes," "no," or "neutral" signals, which we train you to recognize and choose to use for better decisions.

Mind Mastery for 5D Meditation

Higher Self, please inform me of what I need to know,
before I need to know it.

A key takeaway from the Mind Mastery for 5D Meditation: You will gain self-confidence in your Higher Self connection, along with accuracy that you don't have to trust. What's the difference between trusting and knowing? You trust your friend will show up for a lunch date, but you know the sun will come up tomorrow.

Your body is your temple, and that means you may choose to act accordingly, keeping your body in good health with proper fitness, maybe walking outdoors to connect with Mother Earth. Ideally, you will find places you can be barefoot, since that offers the most connection with Earth. You also need proper rest. All of your functions rely on proper rest, including your higher-purpose glands and chakras.

Your pineal gland is the connector to higher states of consciousness. It is widely accepted as one of the body's seven spiritual centers, or chakras. Edgar Cayce said, "Keep the pineal gland operating and you won't grow old. You will always be young!"* One way to proactively give your pineal gland a rest and chance to rejuvenate is to use an eye mask for sleeping during any kind of rest, including naps. This powerful gift of no light to your eyes means that your pineal gland—your gateway to

---

*Cayce readings: 294-141.

spiritual work—is getting the rest and rejuvenation it needs. This means you schedule time for breaks or walks into your busy day, along with naps and enough rest to rejuvenate. Some of you are so busy with your day-to-day chores or work, you push yourself beyond healthy limits for your body, and then can become overtired, which creates stress on all of your four lower bodies, especially your physical body.

The physical body is the experiencer who receives all the information from the three other bodies, and helps you learn who you really are. It is the fullest expression of Source in the physical. Let's make the most of it! This brings us to ascension symptoms. The physical body has three areas of progression: The upper physical body thrives with balanced rest, food, exercise, and time in nature. The middle physical body calibrates with Mother Earth; this is why your connection to your new earthstar chakra (below your feet) is so very important. This is emphasized in numerous of my guided meditations, such as the 5D MerKaBa Meditation* or the Spiral Chakra Meditation.* Your lower physical body is focused on desires such as greed, lust, and avarice. This is where working with the Five Dhyani Buddhas is so helpful.

Certain ascension symptoms are now presenting in your world. Being aware of them will give you peace of mind, even with the discomfort! Ascension symptoms can be extremely mysterious and hard on the body. The following list may be helpful in case your doctors cannot find the cause of your discomfort.

When you cannot determine the cause of these symptoms through traditional doctors or alternative healers, consider that they may be coming from the many upgrades you may be receiving in your body. Remember, your physical body will become the Ascended Master You. Your new crystalline DNA will be brought online. You will not need to die to make this happen.

Symptoms can include headaches due to the expansion of your pineal. You may experience vertigo, dizziness, forgetfulness, joint and body pain or aches, cramps in your legs, changes in your sight and in your awareness of your immediate space. You may feel feverish or flu-like symptoms, cramps, and diarrhea, or even kundalini experiences.

This may result in anxiety attacks that come and go quickly. Many of these upgrades can occur at night, and you might wake up "for no reason" and decide to use the bathroom. This is often a signal that you are "giving permission" to whatever upgrade the ETs of the light may be assisting you with. Announcing "I am waking up well rested no matter what the night holds" will ease this transformation.

Remember that, as a vessel of light, you are being upgraded in many ways. We have chosen this path, albeit painful. One way to address this is to notice this is happening, and to say the following prayer:

> I ask that this divine upgrade assist me and allow me to pursue my highest purpose in this lifetime with the most evolved appearance possible, and expressing in the kindest, most generous, and gentle way. Amen.

Self-care of the physical body is your highest priority right now. Massage, body work, craniosacral work, long baths, etc., will do much for the integration of this new evolved energy. You are becoming 5th-Dimensional. Seek not to understand this new 5D body, but to integrate it with grace and ease.

THE MENTAL BODY

The mental body is an expression of an aspect of you that is often referred to through the Four Lower Bodies. The four lower bodies are representative of certain energy systems connected to the "field"—the vibrational data set also referred to as the matrix. They are also connected to the chakra system, as the chakras receive and supply information from those around you, as well as from the field.

Know that your mental body is alive, with juiciness, like all the four lower bodies. It carefully curates all incoming experience to form a cohesive and coherent whole. To keep your mental body clear keep your thoughts clean and pure and invite uplifting experiences to amplify and intensify your spiritual nature. Your mental body is connected to other peoples' mental bodies because humanity is so very mental these days. For sure, it is not the most important aspect of who you are, but it is an important element that may have become out of balance.

Your mental body is the container of your thoughts. Your thoughts are not you, although many discussions of consciousness indicate that what you think makes you conscious. That may seem backward, but a thinking man is conscious. We do NOT imagine, even if it is so, that animals "think" or have consciousness. We know that when we contemplate our awareness we are accessing consciousness. Our consciousness is mostly contained in the mental body. When we think about ourselves, what we experience emotionally, physically, or energetically impacts consciousness, and is sorted and defined by our mental body.

Humans separate from that which is inseparable in order to expand the consciousness of Source. An important purpose of the mental body is to sort and define all experiences. In this way, we are able to "add to the database." Adding to the database, or collective experiences, is why we incarnate. Otherwise, why bother if you are already part of everything?

Your mental body also helps you form mental images based on your needs and desires, along with the material world you live in. You use your mental body to project your ideas along with your sense of who you are— your identity. This impacts what you think you can do. As you open up to your gifts, your mental body will record those perceptions as well. It is important to remain neutral, and not permit your mind to interpret these subtle experiences but to allow them into the soup of higher consciousness, to meld and blend into your fully awakened self.

Mass consciousness has influenced the mental body and succeeded in programming humankind's mental body. Not everyone is influenced thusly. Mass agreement may cause mass psychosis. Programming transmitted over the airwaves, such as through cell phone antennas or microwave towers, is broadcast nonstop to help you forget who you really are, to consider yourself a God-free being, and to program you to forget the Truth of who you are, focusing instead on anything new that you read about and hear.

But how will you remember who you are? Your primary vehicle to remember your God-Self is meditation. This will enable you to elevate yourself beyond the projections on mass consciousness. This is because mass consciousness mostly exists at a certain frequency. If your frequency is not on the mass-consciousness level (usually around 350–440, according to the David Hawkins scale), and you are above those numbers, then you will not be impacted by broadcasts. Your meditation and other spiritual practices will elevate you beyond those frequencies. You do not need to shield yourself from these broadcasts; instead, elevate yourself beyond them.

Remember that your mental body is receiving these waves like a radio. If you are not tuned to those frequencies, you will not need to be concerned about their impact on you, though you may wish to be aware of their impact on others. Also, it is important to note that your ability to receive and then vibrate at higher frequencies does not make you better than others. This is a false belief that actually lowers your frequency. Look for ways to advance your abilities, so you can broadcast the higher frequencies toward others, elevating them so they may be able to rise above the mass-consciousness programming.

Your mental body is a gateway for information, which you can accept or reject. Humanity is on the cusp of major transformation. You are a wayshower and part of the magic of 5D.

There are many ways humans receive information. They do this through subtle and not so subtle ways. You use your mental body to receive data and sort data. If you allow your mental body to run the show, you will not be able to understand the subtleties of the other receptors of information, such as the Chakras and other lower bodies. Individuals who are highly mental may have difficulty with silent meditation. This is one of the many reasons I've created so many guided meditations.

THE EMOTIONAL BODY

In the esoteric (secret) work, there are at least ten bodies that are part of our creation. These ten bodies are related to the planets and the sephira of the Tree of Life. Because the higher, finer bodies are not affected or influenced adversely by the human condition, I am only discussing the four lower bodies in this chapter.

As emphasized previously, the four lower bodies are affected by human personality. The etheric body is the "body electric," and is related to the Fire element (the other elements are Earth = physical body, Air = mental body, Water = emotional body). According to Joseph Polanski, "Each of these bodies is under the dominion of an Archangel: the etheric body by Archangel Michael, the mental body by Archangel Raphael, the feeling body by Archangel Gabriel, and the physical body by Archangel Uriel."

Gabriel can be called upon to help you balance your emotions. He is the great communicator, having been the messenger that brought the news of pregnancy to both Mother Mary and her cousin Anne. My two meditations to the Seven Archangels can help you with all of your four lower bodies: Rainbow Angel Meditation* has the corresponding biblical references, and the Seven Archangels and the Wheel* is a very healing and proactive reminder of the power found within your requests to the Archangels.

The emotional body is related to the planet Venus—many of us can relate to the well-known book by John Gray, *Men Are from Mars, Women Are from Venus.* Certainly, women seem to be more in touch with our feeling nature, ergo the emotional body, than our fine male counterparts. No matter what your gender, the emotional body deals with a very specific quality of evaluating and expressing reactions to events through emotion. Emotions are chi that you've filled with a purpose. Emotion is the ability to qualify or "color" chi (God Energy) based on your unique God Spark, which makes chi qualified with a specific energy. Qualifying chi into emotion is one of the things that humans do well.

Robert Monroe, founder of the Monroe Institute, named elevated emotional energy *Loosh.* Loosh can be a fuel source for the energies that would have you fail. Loosh, being life force energy (chi, imbued with a purpose), can be either uplifting or down-lowering. The down-lowering loosh refers to the emotional energy radiated by humans and animals who are in dire circumstances. This fear-filled energy is imbued with adrenochrome, which is misused by some. And so, Loosh, in this usage, describes a negative experiential spectrum. However, there is elevating loosh as well, as we will see!

THE DARK SIDE

Loosh from painful and difficult circumstances can be a fuel for the dark forces (not-God energies), since it contains both the God Spark and the human creative spark, and is generated from panic or fear—it's a picnic near an anthill. Do you wonder who you might be feeding when you reexperience some difficult event? You may be feeding an energy that is misusing your light. Some call these dark forces "the powers that were"—emphasis being on the past, and that they are now on the decline.

THE LIGHT SIDE

Our planet is being bathed in uplifting Loosh—helpful, nurturing chi coming directly from sources of love and light, helping humanity transform the planet. This positive Loosh is irresistible and elevating to all of humanity. Clearly intend that you are receiving and animating this positive chi throughout your being, providing you with elevating, heart-expanding energy that YOU can radiate outward.

USES OF MEMORY

Human memory was never intended to re-create agonizing emotions to reexperience our painful pasts. This is why it is useful to develop the habit of only telling your sad story three times. This validates your experience without re-creating the pain of the past. When you count how many times you have told a painful experience, you put a limit on the emotional body reworking your sorrow and disappointment. As a practice, I encourage you to pick the three times you tell your story—not to just deliver it to some random friend that may be calling you when you are upset. You can save your sorry tale for a close friend or family member who will give you the empathy you seek.

All four lower bodies influence each other. The emotional body does seem to have the least number of controls or natural discipline, but each of the four lower bodies can get out of control.

Make no mistake, this hologram we call 3rd Dimension does have both positive and negative emotions. Your goal is to pay attention to your joyful happy moments, laugh and optimize them, and remain balanced at every turn. As you will find in my manifestation book, *Be a Genie*, you can recycle sad, unresolved emotions by practicing two-fers. Two-fers are a way of creating two positives to antidote a negative emotion or thought. Some say you need three—the Losada ratio. But this was disproven by mathematicians who agreed that positive thoughts can outnumber negative ones. Thus, it may require only two positives to antidote a negative emotion.

Your emotions are the strongest of the four lower bodies and can drive your physical and mental health. Memories of sad and painful emotions can re-create the pain of difficult circumstances, making us sick physically or mentally. There are many attempts to influence humans through our devices and airwaves. It is up to each individual to keep your energy above the lower vibrational data sets that can adversely influence you. Control your emotional body by choosing wisely your mental body thoughts through the company you keep, the music and electronic media you pay attention to, and using meditation. This can be done easily if you meditate regularly.

THE ETHERIC BODY

Your etheric body is the source of your beautiful three-fold flame of the heart: love, wisdom, and power. Each and every one of us can receive help from the universe to cleanse, clarify, and magnify our four lower bodies. You might call to the Great Divine Director to align your four lower bodies. Even the Earth has an etheric body, which protects and supports life on this planet.

The etheric body holds memories and experiences throughout your whole lifetime. Initially, it is meant to protect the physical body, and is full of love and light, along with a beautiful blueprint for your lifetimes. It encases your soul when you die. Your etheric body is identified with who you think you are based on your history and experiences. It colors your self-perception.

Yet, over time it can become tainted with pain and trauma you might not have healed. You may wish to practice forgiveness. One such practice is to write a list of people you need to forgive every day for forty-five days. Start with a fresh, clean piece of paper each day, having shredded or burned the prior one. As you progress, day by day, some names will fall off your list, and new ones will appear. This is you clearing out your etheric body! Keep doing this every day for forty-five days. If you forget one day, just pick up where you left off. Finally, if you forget that you forgot, you are done! This does happen!

Another lovely practice that is simple and easy is the Hawaiian practice of forgiveness known as Ho'oponopono, which uses the statements "I'm sorry, please forgive me, I love you, and thank you." This practice is repeated over and over when you are ready to unhook from your own pain and suffering. There are many books and resources to help with this very effective forgiveness practice.

Negative thoughts or a negative view of life also wears down your etheric body, which is the closest to your physical body. This may lead to poor energy or fatigue, or worse—illness. Many of us have carried multiple behaviors from one lifetime to another. We are meant to change the behaviors and learn quickly to disengage from familiar but detrimental patterns to produce a healthy experience, by choosing differently.

How can you fix it? A healthy diet, good exercise, being outside in nature, practicing an energy balancing exercise such as Qi Gong, and of course the forgiveness exercises provided above.

The white fire core at the heart of Source can help you cleanse and clear your etheric body. Can you imagine your three-fold flame filling you with wisdom and compassion? Can you let your newfound awareness of the etheric body as a source of perfected memory reclaim your original blueprint of your three-fold flame? Yes. You can do this today, right NOW. Ask the Master of the Ascension Ray, Serapis Bey, for the ability to do this, asking for his assistance to ensure your success.

Another powerful way to heal the flaws of the etheric body is to repeat a popular violet flame decree, thus: "I am a being of violet fire, I am the purity God desires." Repeat this thirty-six times daily if you can, for maximum results.

Each and every one of you has a home in the etheric plane, your mansion in the sky! You can ask to journey to this special place in your meditations and dream time. Consciously ask to be taken to this wonderful place, your very own mansion in the sky, where you can be refreshed and renewed—especially when you are depressed or suffering from disappointment or despair.

Spend fifteen minutes before bed calling to your Holy Higher Self and the Higher Self of your Twin Flame to reunite on the etheric plane in your mansion in the sky. Prepare to be amazed.

The Mantras for Ascension Meditation* contains two extremely powerful mantras sung as chants that you can sing along to, use to clear your field of excess emotion, and keep your heart open to God. The Hathor Chant will clear the auric field through the four lower elements all the way down to the Earth. It allows you to clear and expand your pranic tube while connecting to Mother Earth. The Kabbalistic (Hebrew) Chant will clear the field through all the dimensions, all realities, all the way back to God. Both are great for clearing your fields of excess emotions.

Once you have brought your well-developed four lower bodies into balance, they can be unified into your human dynamic body of light. This leads to you having balanced the seven lower chakras, the higher chakras (chakras eight to twelve), as well as the Secret Ray Chakras. As your own mastery develops, you become your Ascended Master self.

The Secret Ray Chakras are located on the body at the centers of the palms, the soles of the feet, and near the spleen. These chakras have an "outbound" nature, capable of pushing information instead of pulling it in. This is why hands-on healing holds significant potency. People practicing hands-on healing are essentially projecting energy from their Secret Ray Chakras and the Secret-Ray Elohim mentioned in the prologue. Even nursing babies receive an extra boost when placed next to this chakra during breastfeeding.

This is where humanity is headed, for each one of us to become an Ascended Master, alive in our physical bodies, utilizing all of our God-given powers. You no longer need to die to be an Ascended Master!

THE CELESTIAL SOUL

Your Celestial Soul, or Oversoul, is the "father/mother" of its children. Each Oversoul is the master identity that oversees its many subdivisions in many realities.* When you meet someone and have an instant connection, maybe feeling like you've known each other forever, you are probably talking to a soul mate, or "other expression" of your Oversoul. All Oversouls together have descended from Source collectively. They produce the Christ Consciousness. A twin soul is an energy that descends from Source and immediately splits into two equal parts.

Activating your High Heart Chakra is one of the most important things you can do to advance your spiritual growth. You may have already been using your High Heart Chakra if you've been experiencing third eye opening or Kundalini activation. Your High Heart Chakra is located in the seat of the thymus gland. It is the gateway that connects you to Source.

One way to activate the thymus is through using the Secret Ray Chakras of your hand, lightly touching the center of the palm to activate it and inviting unconditional love to flood in, through, and around the thymus. You may add crystals if you have them—kyanite is a great choice, as is green calcite—by placing them in the center of your palm,

---

*The Healer's Handbook: A Journey into Hyperspace by Stewart Swerdlow, page 137.

then placing your palm over the thymus with the crystal touching your skin. It does not matter if the crystal if raw or polished. If you do not have a crystal, you may write the name of the crystal on a small piece of paper, make a clear intention that you are using the law of correspondence (allowing something to stand in for something else). First, locate the thymus on the body. It is just below the clavicle bones, in the center above your sternum. It may protrude a bit as a roundish bump. Not everyone's thymus protrudes this way. In the early evolution after the person is born, the thymus plays an important role, creating T cells that can be used anywhere to support the body's immune functions. As you mature, the physical jobs of the thymus become less active. This is when your spiritual aspects begin to take root. When you send energy to your thymus, you are bringing in lightforce energy—imagine it like back-flushing a filter. If you could see it, it might resemble black smoke exiting blood vessels.

... 9 ...

What's the Next Opportunity?

To take a line from *Mastering Your 5D Self,* "Putting an end to evil does not require that the evil ones be punished. It means purging that energy from the system so that it can never wreak havoc again!"[*] One of the hardest things for people to grasp is that worrying about "those that deserve" punishment—or worse—keeps you locked in to the old game. Those who would have you fail are delighted that you are so concerned!

It's time. It's time to move into your place of unconditional love. When you are stuck, depressed, or in a place of procrastination, try reciting this mantra: "Dear God, show me how much I am loved." Life on this planet can be strange and unpredictable. You may face many crazy events in the next few months or years. The Heart Countdown Meditation[♦] will help you hold your own and stay connected to your heart of unconditional love, your High Heart Chakra.

This meditation is the result of a simple countdown, originally created at the beginning of the COVID pandemic lockdowns, so we could stay out of fear. Since then, I've rerecorded it, so it's even easier to move into a heart space, and I do the counting for you! Sometimes all you need is for someone to talk you off the ledge.

---

[*]*Mastering Your 5D Self,* by Maureen J. St. Germain, page 88.

Heart Countdown Meditation

We ask the angelic realm to activate our inner awarenes and
help us remember what to ask for!

A key takeaway from the Heart Countdown Meditation: The skill
of centering yourself through a countdown from ten to one involves
assigning each number to a specific aspect of life, like altruism, self-love,
parental love, the absence of parental love, and even down to the cham-
bers within the heart and what they represent.

This is a good time to be reminded of the value of two more of my favorite tools to help you stay in 5th Dimension. The first is to state daily:
"I am asking for a day of heaven on Earth, for me and everyone I'm in
contact with, and everyone I am in contract with!" This key phrase will
change everything for you, and will improve all your communications
with everyone you talk to! My other favorite tool to use when going to
sleep is: "I am waking up in 5D." This announcement to yourself and
your Angels and Guides sets the intention for the day to come.

All of my guided meditations will uplift you and help heal certain
issues you may be encountering. My basics, aside from the MerKaBa
and 5D MerKaBa, are the Angel Meditations* and the Crystal Elohim
Meditation.* If you have time, I invite you to also practice the Golden
Bowl Meditation* in order to amp up your connection to Source. This
meditation may open your sinuses, as many users have reported, giving
you physical proof of the opening of the sinus cavity bowl, the unique
energy vehicle to connect with Source. You work so hard to become
5th-Dimensional, and with these tools you are able to be your 5th-
Dimensional self effortlessly.

If you have ever felt like your Higher Self connection needed a
boost, my Illuminate app has full instructions to connect with your
Higher Self—in fact, this information is so important, it is featured in
all of my books. Using this connection on a regular basis will assist you
in creating that space and awareness of your Higher Self. I hope you
enjoy it!

WORKING WITH WHAT YOU DON'T KNOW

I have a friend whose family home burned to the ground on Christmas Day. Her father, a psychiatrist, had thought it would be safe to burn Christmas wrapping paper in the fireplace. Built-up creosote in the chimney caught fire first, and then the flaming paper floated up and out of the chimney and landed on the roof. The roof caught fire quickly, and the house was gone—burned to the ground in less than thirty minutes. My friend commanded her dad to leave the burning house, as he had no idea the danger they were in! He didn't know what he didn't know! They managed to get out of their house . . . but barely.

When you don't know what you don't know, you can be missing opportunities—and more. This is an important subject for all of us to understand. In an important study done in 1999, researchers Dunning and Kruger* found two key areas of overestimating what you know. The first group I want to talk about is the group that knows a little about a subject or area and tends to underestimate their abilities, probably because they recognize the vastness of the subject matter. They are on a learning-and-listening track. The other two groups, those with low cognitive scores think they have more knowledge and comprehension than they do. Their self-evaluation is higher than it should be. The other group, experts in a field of knowledge, tend to assume others know what they know and make the mistake of having higher expectations for everyone.

Do you have a friend who is telling you your situation is dire, that you are living in denial just wishing it will fix itself? Pay attention. If you do not act when your guidance talks to you—or your like-minded friends do—you may have a setback! You may sustain losses. Perhaps those losses may be necessary to get you to wake up to your deficiencies.

*See the Dunning-Kruger effect article on Ness Labs website.

LETTING GO

Not all letting go will be a celebration, but any letting go will make an improvement in your life. As you look at your own life and your beliefs, policies and attitudes may need a makeover. Choose to let go of your need to be right. Choose to let go of your old ways of doing things. When there's a new and better way, don't resist the change just because it requires you to learn new things.

Our world is filled with so many material possessions, some families have created a special "gifting day" with their children, to let the child choose what to keep and what to give away. They call it "make room for new toys." In this way, letting go becomes a joyful celebration!

When you get a new car, you must let go of your old one. Sometimes that's a treasured vehicle. Learning to operate the new car and familiarize yourself with its updated features requires effort. Some of your knowledge will be transferable, some of it won't. However, enjoying the ability to go places in your new car lets you really relax into it. You can learn the new tools with enthusiasm.

During this time of renewal and breakthrough, please give yourself time to relax, to regroup, and to rethink your priorities. Your life is important. You are important. You will want to stick around for the upleveling of humanity. Remember, someone has to uplevel first—it may as well be you! The tide has gone out—be ready for the incoming! There are souls who have already moved into 5D permanently, and they are holding the balance for the rest of humanity to find their way. Once the ability to move into that space permanently is acquired, a road map or energetic imprint can follow.

SOUL RETRIEVAL

The purpose of soul retrieval is to reclaim lost parts of yourself that you may have broken off in order to survive a trauma. During your life you may purposefully break off pieces of yourself in order to break free from the pain and suffering these big emotions carry, much like an animal will chew off a leg that is caught in a trap. Your broken-off pieces can land anywhere, but generally can be found near to the location of the original event. This reunification practice is a significant tradition of Native peoples in the United States. Sandra Ingerman has been considered one of the world's authorities on this subject for over thirty years. I was a student of this material in the '80s, but never did anything with it.

When my younger sister was killed in a car crash in France, I was in Hawaii teaching a class involving swimming with dolphins. My mother also happened to be living in Hawaii at that time, and we traveled together to Paris for the funeral. I left many parts of myself along that journey (a big story), and chose to postpone all my classes for about six weeks in order to fully grieve and not fall apart while teaching. One day, I was given explicit directions from my Guides for calling back my lost soul parts from all the trauma I had experienced (on top of the tragedy of my sister's passing, the airline couldn't find my passport—which my son had delivered from my lockbox to the airport, some eighty miles away, to give to an airline employee who carried it on her flight to Houston, Texas, to then be delivered to me in Houston—for my connection to Paris!). Unity! A Soul Retrieval Meditation* was the result of that instruction!

Unity! A Soul Retrieval Meditation

Before bedtime, say out loud: "I am requesting my Higher Self to journey to moments in time and space where I may have fragmented parts of myself. I seek the retrieval of these aspects, bringing them into my aura for complete clearing and integration tomorrow." Remember to clear and then "bathe" your recovered parts in love before welcoming them into your field. In the morning, affirm: "I now call upon Archangel Raphael to envelop my recovered parts with a healing balm for their full integration. I also invoke Archangel Michael to encircle me with a protective blue energy until the integration process is complete."

A key takeaway from the Unity! A Soul Retrieval Meditation: The ability to do soul retrieval by yourself, for yourself. You don't need to find a practitioner of soul retrieval in order to recover your lost soul parts.

✳

A friend and participant of the dolphin swim, who was with me when I learned the news of my sister's passing, called me almost daily while I was in Paris to see how I was doing. The day of my soul retrieval, he announced, "Maureen, you sound like you're all back together!"

And I was.

MEMORY LINKS

Sometimes a missing part of us can be connected to a memory. Memory links can be found in time and space, connected to the specific trauma. Therefore, traveling through time or space allows you to access it. The coordinates for these memories also exist in time and space. There are three possible options for opening one of these portals to tunnel through and open up another time and place in order to connect with a prior trauma, but only two are required. When you drive past the physical location of an old memory, the trauma can resurface. If you think about the past and feel your emotion, this gives you the ability to connect with that time. The three possible options: are location, you, and memories or some other time-related trigger, like an anniversary date.

In the movie *Somewhere in Time*, actor Christopher Reeve provides us with a wonderful and dramatic portrayal of a man going into the past using the depth of his emotion tied to memories that allow him to open a portal to another time and place.

If you have ever visited a place where there was great travail and suffering, such as some of the Native American monuments, battlefields, or places where tragic events have occurred, you may have experienced those energies and feelings.

While driving past the Experimental Aircraft Association

Aviation Museum in Oshkosh, Wisconsin, I tapped into the huge "disappointment energy" of someone dear to me, who had driven there only to be turned away because he didn't have the full entrance fee, which was over his budget. I knew of his experience, yet I had no memory of it as I approached this location. All of a sudden, I was hit with a huge sadness. I could feel his deep disappointment. It was a very sad time for him in general, and his dissatisfaction with his life was reaffirmed by his disappointment at spending several hours driving to this wonderful museum, only to be turned away due to insufficient funds. Driving past this location, on a road that I had not traveled in over ten years, along with my connection to this young man, caused his wound to be palpable to my heart. A poignant moment, to say the least. But I realized that my connection to this friend and his situation could help to heal his trauma. You may have had similar events, where you were not the direct recipient of the trauma or disappointment, but feel you could have influenced it for someone else. The Unity! A Soul Retrieval Meditation* will provide the tools to heal this.

Many years ago, while driving a small car crossing a mountain pass, the car spun out on black ice, landing in a high snow bank. I was with one of my sons. We were not injured, nor was the car damaged, although we did need a tow truck to pull the car out of the snow bank. It was eventful yet relatively harmless. We took a vacation day for the rest of the day, instead of our usual seventy-five-mile Monday morning trek to the city where I worked and he attended school.

Thirteen years later, on a remarkably similar route, this same son was driving cross-country, moving with his girlfriend to a new city. His route took him over the same mountain pass, this time in the summer, past the site of the car accident that he and I had experienced thirteen years earlier, when he'd been just eleven years old. He called me on the phone, and said, "Did something happen with us on that mountain pass?" As he drove by the site, its connection to him surfaced without him remembering the reason why. Again, crosshairs of the conditions, location, and his proximity opened the portal to that significant event.

PORTAL OPENINGS

You can physically travel to a place that has great sadness, and if you have a connection to it and openness to receive it, you will sense it. This connection may consist of a past life, where you may have been the original experiencer. This means your connection to it allows you to feel the past trauma. This also mean you can help clear the trauma by allowing the feelings of sadness and hopelessness into your consciousness, where you can feel the anguish, process it, love it, and release it. This is true healing, which means to make whole.

Healing is particularly important for families who've experienced car accidents or other hugely significant trauma or drama. A trauma's coordinates in time and space usually lock it in place, and its link to you and your family make it accessible when you go to the location or visit it in time, through your memory.

WHERE DO YOU GO TO RETRIEVE YOUR LOST PARTS?

All of humanity has learned to let go of the strong emotions that occur due to traumas. You may typically release a chunk of yourself when you let go of a strong emotion because you might not be able to express all of the emotion resulting from a deeply disturbing experience. Your emotion can be stored in your lost parts. As you restore yourself, you heal and become mentally healthy again. Yet, a chunk of you may be lost, managing the unexpressed emotion from that event. Like a trail of breadcrumbs, traveling to the funeral of a loved one may cause you to leave a trail of emotional chunks along the physical path you took.

If your loved one died suddenly, the shock and trauma may be so great that you leave a lot of yourself behind. As you work through the processes of bringing back your lost soul parts, think of this tool as a way to bring everything back together. You will be sending your Higher Self to visit every place you were, from the time you heard the terrible news to the time you finally accepted the sad event. Every place you have told your story, you may have left a piece of yourself in that location.

The retrieval is done in the dream time while you sleep. After this instruction, your Higher Self will bring all the lost parts back to you, where you will "wash" them energetically and reinstall them into you. I recommend that you do the first two meditations (of four found in Unify!) right before bedtime, instructing your Higher Self to travel on your behalf to retrieve your lost parts. The following morning, you will need to complete your ceremony by washing and reintegrating your lost-and-now-found parts through the remaining two meditations.

Please remember, if you left a part of yourself behind as a form of survival, there is no reason to condemn yourself or any other family member for doing this. Your clear intention while performing this retrieval will open up those links and let you become more of who you are. Your memory of the event serves as one link to the location of a lost part. Being in the physical location is another way to connect with it. The Unity! A Soul Retrieval Meditation* will take you through this process.

When you retrieve a lost part of yourself, you will free up the emotions related to the incident. Emotions are energy in matter. This freed-up energy can then be used elsewhere in your life. This allows you to be less dependent on mass consciousness to "complete you," and inspires the authentic you to emerge. Peoples' capacity to create with emotion is far greater than you ever thought possible. Your job is to heal your emotional wounds, which then heals planet Earth and all those upon her. Mother Earth is not healed by your judgments, but with your love. Doing the Unity! A Soul Retrieval Meditation* for yourself after a big loss is one way to heal yourself and our planet. Please consider waiting about six weeks from any trauma before performing the following ceremony and meditation.

We asked members of our Ascension Institute to do the Unity! A Soul Retrieval Meditation* every night for a week or two—not to address a specific trauma, but to recover from prior events that perhaps didn't seem important. When we began to cyclically do soul retrieval each night, we discovered that we may be retrieving lost parts from other lifetimes! Some of us have retrieved lost parts from outside this reality, from events we did not know about or remember! Another thing you need to comprehend is the presence of entities and other energies that may be attempting to interfere. There are off-planet energies which may have collected samples of your DNA, or your skin. They use these biological samples to clone you, or create other energies. They are using soul shards from humans to create false timelines—and alternate versions of you! You can reclaim these through your own soul retrieval work, until you feel you have recovered all your lost parts.

TIME AND PLACE

Remember, it takes three possible conditions to create a vortex or portal to tunnel through and open up to another time and place. The three possible options are: location, you, and memories or other time-related events. Again, you only need two of these points, like the crosshairs on a scope, or an intersection. Think of a boat moving through water, creating a wake on either side of it. The meeting of the two wakes, or conditions, causes a spin (see the image below). The spin (curved arrow) creates a vortex because it is ties to a specific time and place, and the spin opens that portal.

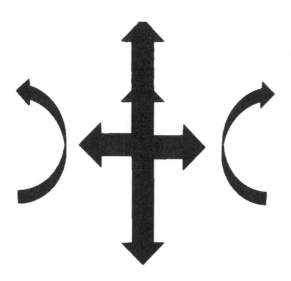

Scientifically, this has been proven with the art of radiesthesia, initially discovered by a group of French geomancy researchers who studied non-visible energy flow. French radiesthesists in the 1940s refer to the compression wave that creates a specific quality in a specific angle to magnetic north. I have discovered that any two of these signatures can cause a vortex to appear. Russian scientist Dr. N. A. Kozyrev proved this by identifying compression waves that move faster than the speed of light!

According to Ibrahim Karim, Ph.D., D.Sc., "In multidimension physics of quality within BioGeometery they have identified several levels of emotional, mental and higher compression wave planes that travel faster than light and are not confined by the limits of time and space. The waves and matter in those dimensions follow different laws."*

These counterrotating fields create the vortex that opens the portal to the event or experience so that you might discover and heal it using the Unity! A Soul Retrieval Meditation.◆

Biogeometry Signatures, Ibrahim Karim, Ph.D., Dr, Sc.

···10···

Cleaning and Clearing Your Twelve DNA Strands and Chakras

There is much discussion about the origins of the human and the human soul. This chapter will hopefully give insight and understanding of the magnitude of our human creation.

Anyone can channel higher beings. Your accurate Higher Self connection will be able to help you sort through that. Many people are channeling—but are they all higher beings? No! A person can be hijacked by entities with agendas that are counter to the process of spiritual evolution. I am discovering that many people who have been channeling higher beings, or their Higher Self, have discovered quite innocently that they have been inadvertently channeling dark energies. Could this be you?

In one case, a woman I met on a cruise I was recently on told me she was a big fan of my work, and didn't need to participate in my Ascension Institute, as she had read all my books and put them to work for herself, and had a big connection with her Higher Self. I asked if she had her Higher Self connection going. She said yes, so I congratulated her and wished her well. She didn't seem to be seeking my advice at that time, even though she was thrilled to meet me.

Later that same week, she came back to me very upset. She'd had a reading with someone who informed her that she was channeling a dark energy—which is why I'd asked about her Higher Self connection! I don't know if she was looking to me to repudiate the other channeler or not, but I told her I'd thought the same when I'd met her. Since she hadn't asked my opinion in that first conversation, I didn't feel it was my place to share my suspicions.

This has been happening to me over and over in the past six months. Maybe, in the excitement to be a conveyor of otherworldly messages, individuals are inadvertently allowing "frauds" to take the place of their Higher Self. We keep getting calls from people who don't understand what's going on for them—until they speak with us and it comes out!

Now it's time for your own safety check. Even if you think you're bringing in really good information, it could still be an entity setting you up to follow or believe everything it may tell you. Your Higher Self will never tell you to break the law or do anything unkind toward anyone. Nor will it advise you to do something you know will hurt you or someone else. But your Higher Self can and will advise you, counterintuitively, to take action when your ego doesn't want to.

For example, when I was still working in my corporate job, my Higher Self told me to call the reporter who covered my subject area when I was trying to get a story about my nonprofit in the news.

I responded back to my Higher Self, "No, it's almost five at night—I want to go home and eat dinner, I'm hungry."

Again, my Higher Self directed me to make the call.

I was thinking, "I've called this guy a half dozen times all day with no results. Besides, my kids are waiting for me to fix dinner!"

A third time I heard, "Call the reporter" from my Higher Self.

I've learned over the years that it's OK to argue with your Higher Self, but if the instruction arrives three times, take the action you're told to take.

I called the reporter. Amazingly, he answered the phone! "Maureen, how could you possibly know I would be here at this time—I'm never here at this time!"

All I could do was laugh, since I wasn't about to tell him my Higher

Self had insisted! The best part is, my story made the front page of the largest newspaper in the state the following morning!

How can you know for sure if your Higher Self is giving you the guidance you receive? You can ask. You can go through the Higher Self Protocol for six weeks, and then every time information comes in, you can ask, "Higher Self, is this my Higher Self telling me to _____?" Fill in the blank with the action step you were given.

Your Higher Self is YOU. Your Higher Self is plugged into the cosmos and you, and knows what you care about as well as what's going on around you. The earlier times I'd called the reporter with no result, I hadn't thought about checking in with my Higher Self, yet my Higher Self was tuned in to my need to get in touch with him, and gave me the precise time to call to make that happen.

Do you always follow through with what your Higher Self tells you? If not, you do not truly trust your Higher Self, and are just following its instruction when convenient! If you cannot answer "100 percent of the time," then you really don't believe your Higher Self is your Higher Self! Maybe you have a strong ego. If that is true, do another six weeks of practicing the Higher Self Protocol, checking on unimportant things (I will explain in just a moment) to give you another round of positive data—this will prove that your Higher Self is always right.

How else will you know whether you have a good connection with your Higher Self? The only way to prove to yourself that you have a good connection, and that you haven't been hacked, is to do the Higher Self Protocol. Six easy, fun weeks of practice, asking only about unimportant steps to take.

◆ Higher Self Protocol
The goal of this practice is to learn your Higher Self's signals for "yes," "no," and "neutral."

✦ Discover Your Higher Self's Signals
Shut your eyes and open your heart. Welcome your Higher Self into your heart space. Request three symbols or signals to signify Yes, No, and

Neutral. These symbols might appear as colors or shapes in your mind, sensations in your body, or even the explicit words *Yes, No,* or *Neutral.* Typically, these signals manifest spontaneously. A few individuals may require a workaround. Even if your signals are subtle, trust them until they become more recognizable to you.

✦ Step 1: Ask Questions

Start by asking: "Higher Self, is it in my highest and best good to take this action (filling in the action step you are considering)?" Always ask about things you are willing to do. Don't "test" your Higher Self by asking predictive questions, or things you are not willing to do. Don't ask about eating meat if you are a committed vegan. Don't ask about quitting smoking during your six weeks of this protocol.

✦ Step 2: Take Action

Once you understand your Higher Self's signals, by going into meditation and asking your Higher Self for your Yes, No, and Neutral, then play with your Higher Self for the next six weeks with unimportant, insignificant actions. Good questions to ask would be what clothes to wear, routes to take, food to eat, etc.

✦ Step 3: Avoid Other Divination Tools

Be playful, don't ask questions about anything important, and set aside your pendulum or other divination tools. Always follow through. If you ask your Higher Self about a yummy-looking dessert and your Higher Self says "No, tell the waitress, 'No, thank you'!" The goal of this step is to combine listening to your Higher Self's instruction and putting that instruction into practice. Repeat this step for six weeks.

✦ Step 4: Completing Your Six-Week Practice

After six weeks of this protocol, new DNA kicks in, and you'll have put a good pattern into place. Then you won't have to trust your Higher Self, you'll *know* that your Higher Self always has your back. Your Higher Self always will give you the ideal answer, even when your personality thinks otherwise.

So, what are you waiting for? If you already know this and do this, then tell your friends!

CLEARING INFORMATION

Your physical body is your highest priority right now. No matter what you believe or know, taking good care of your physical body will give you the strength to face all kinds of challenges. Originally, the human body was designed to be self-healing, and to live for hundreds of Earth years. Some will tell you aging is because you've misused your free will, and that you must deal with aging. However, I've been shown that our "Self-healing DNA" was disconnected from our DNA spiral. You can reclaim this by knowing the missing DNA are in a lower dimension, and you can ask for them to wake up and phase up to where you are now, in order for your DNA structure to expand and grow. This will greatly change how you age! Also check out our annual Youthing Event, held on the full harvest moon each year, usually in September.

At our Ascension Institute, we have many tools to help you manage your self, and your traumas and dramas. As humanity emerges from the many challenges of the past, know that you can and will emerge wiser, happier, and more self-aware than before. Claim this. Here is a prayer you may use for clearing, excerpted from the Bedtime Prayer:

I now command bolts of God's crystalline light to blaze in, through, and around my self-healing DNA strands, and to wake up and phase up to where I am. To cleanse, heal, activate, and integrate them into my DNA structure, allowing them to expand and grow. This will speed up the self-healing process, and allow them to serve me where I am. I now command my Higher Self to assist me in rearranging my molecules to harmonize with my new awareness and understanding of time and space. This allows me to shift dimensionally with grace and ease. This permits me to move my awareness beyond my current dimension, to allow my focus in more than one dimension, and to remember my experiences. I let go and release all of my prior genetic programming. I command my Higher Self to locate the highest vibrational frequency that my body has ever had. I command my Higher Self to locate, energize, and reattach it. I command my Higher Self to connect to my DNA and to each of the sixty-four codons that make up the full spectrum of my DNA, to increase to their highest frequency. I open my heart to receive the highest DNA activation possible.

We've been doing a lot of Quantum Matrix Healing work here at the Ascension Institute, using this tool to change undesired behaviors and patterns, and level them up to their most evolved expression as defined by the Higher Self. This practice has created some amazing outcomes. Yet, some who have attempted this work on their own have fallen prey to dark energies. It's possible to be influenced by energies with opposing agendas. They might deceive you by providing accurate information initially, and then subtly inserting false information that doesn't quite feel right. You might be tempted to assume, "Well, all the other information I received was accurate, so this must be accurate too!"

Because there seems to be many more dark energies surfacing as the veils become thinner, you may not realize you've opened yourself to unwanted influences. One student began channeling an entity that, after a year or so, demanded that he return to his "home" planet to save their planet. The whole thing climaxed when he claimed that he must leave this Earth that night. His father rushed home and saw that his son had a very low pulse and was pale white—like he was dying. His father, an atheist, urged him not to believe in all of this. He was terrified his son would die that night!

Finally, the son agreed to stay on Earth, and the whole thing backlashed. The kingdom he was channeling from accused him of being a traitor and attacked him. He'd been fighting off their attack for days, waving knives nonstop to try to clear these unseen attackers, when he reached out to me.

I asked this man to call in K-17 (the code name for the head of the

Cosmic Secret Service) for assistance, along with Archangel Michael, and to do clearing work. K-17, an Ascended Master, supervises the Divine Plan on Earth. His role involves revealing forces and plots that could jeopardize human sovereignty on Earth.* For those of you who want to know how to do this, you can watch and learn as you check out our YouTube channel for do-it-yourself instructions. If you feel your issue is too big to clear yourself, you can also hire our clearing team for assistance.

Additionally, you are allowed to clear family members even without their permission. This is because these energies are not allowed to be here on the Earth at this time. Even though they were part of this reality at one time, they must take their exit. Even though they know their time is up, they haven't been "kicked out" until a human does this. These entities and energies will take advantage of you or family members by creating havoc, and then living off your emotional energy, called loosh. Loosh was discussed in chapter 8.

I recommend that you NOT clear children directly, as they will copy you and try to clear their friends. Can you imagine the conversation you would have in the principal's office? Children may be cleared remotely, ideally while they are out of the house or sound asleep. Be prepared, as they can wake up while you are doing this, which is why you may want to wait until they're out of the house. They will be different after a clearing—and it will be a good thing! I have a story of one family who cleared a troublesome six-year-old at their daughter's preschool—the parents and children at the preschool were afraid of this child's behavior! She was verbally abusive to the other parents, including using foul language, and her parents did not know what to do. The clearing ceremony was done, and the child reverted to her true, sweet self! The drama stopped.

Random pains in the body need to be addressed. People who are ill or homebound may experience unexplainable pains that are not related

---

*You can also look at pages 50 and 51 of *Mastering Your 5D Self,* which has an explanation.

to a known illness. They may have reported these things to their doctor or caregivers, with no explanation forthcoming. If you or someone you know has random unexplained pain, it may very well be an entity taking advantage of your overall state. All pains need to be checked out by a medical professional. However, if a random pain comes to you, do not assume it is from a benevolent source or some part of your estranged body. You can even do clearing work while you are waiting for a callback from the doctor! Entities are taking advantage of humans, and you have a right to demand they leave, using the following phrase: "If you are not of 100 percent God light, you must leave. If you are 100 percent God light, you may stay."

If the pain persists, do see a doctor. Everyone has the opportunity and obligation to expand their spirituality—everyone on the planet can help save the planet. Our technology has outpaced our spirituality. The universe is waiting for humanity to catch up.

◆ Advanced Clearing, the Monad, and 144,000 Oversouls

Remember a time when you've held a little one—a pet or an infant—in your arms. Hear yourself say, "I love you" to the little one, three times. With your heart open, reach up your pranic tube and invite your Higher Self to connect with you. Now, go to the highest version of you that you can, and connect with that. Let yourself be filled with expansive white light.

Invite the highest-frequency Masters, Angels, and Guides you work with, and connect with them, asking them to step in and work with you. Let them fill you with even more light.

Now, move your attention to your monad, wherever it might be. You have 144 tendrils—not all of them in embodiment here on Earth. You might feel it or see it, but your intention is enough. Working with your entire being, along with Archangel Michael and your team (your Ascended Master Team may include the Masters you work with, such as Djwal Khul, El Morya, St. Germain, Mother Mary, Quan Yin, Mary Magdalene, the Hathors, etc.) to bring clearing, cleansing energy to your monad.

Command your divine-self monad to unhook from any outside systems that may be connected to it, mechanical and nonmechanical, along with any contracts that may be keeping them in place (from this life or past lives), including outside influences. Clear any karmic connections, from any level of existence or imprint on your monad, and bring in more cleansing, clearing energy to your monad, with your entire team of Guides present.

Now, request your team of Angels and Guides to purify and remove the smog enveloping your monad, clearing away all the energy that doesn't belong and is attempting to hinder or obscure the connection to you or your monad. Ask your Ascended Master Team to locate any dark entities or energies that are hovering around. See that all unwanted energies or entities are being picked up and escorted to a place of evolution or dissolution. Now, call in the Ashtar Command, requesting Commander Ashtar to escort any ETs or ET influences from your monad to an appropriate location, and to remove any implants, hooks, or drains.

As you do that, your monad will start to shift colors a little bit, and the frozen energy around it will start to release. Your Angels and Guides are cleansing, clearing, rescinding, and revoking any contracts or connections to any dark sources or source systems, unhooking any hooks or drains, energy cords, or implants of foreign programming or reverse programming, and bringing in more cleansing and clearing to your monad.

Now, call in your galactic Guides, who are bringing love of the highest frequency into, through, and throughout your monad. As this energy comes through, it blasts away anything that doesn't belong, transmuting it to the highest vibrational frequency.

You may observe that anything that was hidden and tucked away is now vibrating to a higher frequency, from the center core out, emanating and pulsing—charging up with this high-frequency energy. And now your monad feels clean and whole.

Now, invite your Guides and Higher Self to assist you in moving your monad to its proper location for you. It may be close to you, it may be in you. Allow that transition to occur. Allow your monad to arrive at the appropriate location for you.

And when you feel like it's in its ideal location you, bring the highest vibrational light into your heart, and allow this energy to fill every part of you and your monad, and to then establish roots, pathways, and connections to you, in a healthy, balanced, wise way.

As this energy of unconditional love and light is rewiring you and filling in connections to you, allow these energies to centralize, balance, and stabilize within yourself and your monad.

When you are ready, bring attention back into the room, opening your eyes when you're ready.

Thinking in 5D Practice

A *Course in Miracles*, written in 1976 by Helen Schucman, states that forgiveness is no longer necessary. *A Course in Miracles* was written long before 5D was ever mentioned or written about in common culture. Yet, the message is clearly 5D. Score keeping is not the same as tracking progress. Score keeping implies that there are winners and losers, or good and bad. Tracking progress means you are aware of where you are at, and self-accepting when you analyze your own choices! If you know when you could have done better, and wish you had, we have a guided meditation for that called the Reality Remix Meditation.* This is a very powerful guided meditation that provides the opportunity for a "do-over," and that can help you transpose a new, "more ideal" choice into THIS reality. It changes your memory, your past, and then produces a domino effect on the present. Seeing the effect in real time is profound.

We no longer need to keep score. No more karma means that you and I are not keeping score on each other or ourselves. This is a monumental leap from how we have interpreted this reality up to now. It's a game changer for sure. How do we navigate this? We do this one small step at a time. The tide has gone out, your karmic entanglements can no longer pull you out into the sea of drama, misinformation, and mistakes. You are now free from the "ocean of permission," where your power was taken away, or you gave it away, possibly, during an inadvertent surrender.

That "sea of drama" can tug and pull on you like the temptation of a freshly opened snack (think of your favorite crunchy snack). To balance this pull, say to yourself, "I'm done with the game, and I'm eager to move into the role of personal responsibility, humility, and love." Let each us find our way through this amazing transition.

Trust plays an important part in this release of karma. Initially, you will need to trust others, even when you suspect their intentions are not of the highest order. It's OK to trust, but verify. And as we become 5th-Dimensional, we choose to "not judge" what others are doing. Choosing to accept others' behavior is positive progress! It does not mean we allow others to hurt us or rob from us.

How do we do this when we've had many affronts toward us, and our reactions may be the hundred-dollar response for the ten-cent problem? For sure, we can enlist the help of the angels. The AroMandala-Orion Series blends of essential oils will greatly assist in self-examination, growth, and change. The thirty-minute Angels meditations (either Rainbow Angel Meditation* or the Seven Archangels and the Wheel Meditation*) will take you through a dozen human foibles. The Five Dhyani Buddhas Meditation* will help you with the five human poisons (mentioned on page xi) and replace them with the highest expression possible.

Rainbow Angel Meditation

I ask each of the seven Archangels to assist me this day in whatever I may need.

A key takeaway from the Rainbow Angel Meditation: You'll discover biblical references to Angels for those who appreciate them. During the meditation, there are pauses for you to make your own requests to the Angels. Each of the seven Archangels brings specific gifts, offering a lovely opportunity to learn about them and make specific requests.

With this tool, you can claim, "I love forgiving." And pretty soon, forgiving won't even be a necessary step. "I love" becomes the operative thought.

Many people do not realize that there are multiple versions of themselves.* These multiple versions are role-playing all the choices that we didn't take. Sometimes you will fantasize about a choice you did not take—a lost relationship, a different job, a different school. You may think about what you would have done if you'd known some important detail about what another person was doing, as some version of you (that is now falling away) has probably already done that! Instead, know that your highest and best choice will serve you in the long run, taking you closer to your 5D self, even when you cannot imagine what that might look like. The age of retaliation is over.

I remember ruminating, "When will he learn to appreciate me?" about a son I was putting through college. When my Guides told me, "When he's twenty-eight," I laughed out loud. Surely he would appreciate me by next week, not four years from now! My discovery was that I was still holding an expectation that had become a barrier to my heart's desire. So I dropped the barrier and let go of the need to be appreciated by him. I reminded myself that I was paying for his college because I wanted to give him that gift. So, let me ask you, "When will you learn to forgive and appreciate blessed YOU?" As you review your past choices, remember to add a little bit of forgiveness to each of the memories that you replace. This will serve to lessen that memory of the old version, and anchor in the new one! For sure, the Reality Remix Meditation* will change the way you look at the past and present.

Reviewing the list of words in *Waking Up in 5D*, a commonly utilized phrase, "I'm sorry," becomes, "Are you OK?"

Have you ever observed a child/parent interaction something like this: A parent, trying to rectify a situation, says, "Say you're sorry."

No answer from the child.

"Say you're sorry," the parent repeats, this time a little louder.

The child hangs her head, but still refuses.

"Say you're sorry!" yells the parent.

Waking Up in 5D, 148.

You want to cringe just watching. Teaching a child to say they are sorry creates an inappropriate power struggle. The "victim" is now in power, and the child must submit! Far more appropriate to the times we are moving into is when we recognize that we all are doing the best we can—we are all becoming ascended (whether we want to or not)—and that saying you're sorry to anyone creates an unequal relationship.

What if we taught children to say, "Are you OK?" This would allow the "victim" to express their wound and how they are feeling. Then the perpetrator child can show empathy or concern, rather than disdain or defensiveness. Teaching and expecting children to have empathy or compassion is part of developing the Empathy Response. It is the new 5D way.

No one "has to" anything. This means your voice is important and you can choose to resist politely. To do this, list your need and then invite cooperation. "I need to keep our house tidy and clean because it makes me happy. I need you to help by picking up after yourself."

In a 2012 study* published in the *Journal of Consumer Research*, researchers split 120 students in two groups. One group was trained to use the phrase "I can't" when discussing specific choices, while the other was trained to use "I don't" in framing their decisions.

The students who told themselves "I can't eat 'X'" chose to eat the chocolate candy bar 61 percent of the time. Meanwhile, the students who told themselves "I don't eat 'X'" chose to eat the chocolate candy bars only 36 percent of the time. This simple change in terminology significantly improved the odds that each person would make a healthier food choice.

When you say "I don't do something," you are owning the action. When you use "I can't," you are implying there is someone that is keeping score who won't let you do it! Next time you need to avoid saying "yes," use "I don't" in your refusal, to reinforce the helpful behavior of saying "no" to things that aren't worth it.

---

*Patrick, Vanessa M., and Henrik Hagtvedt. "'I Don't' versus 'I Can't': When Empowered Refusal Motivates Goal-Directed Behavior." *Journal of Consumer Research* 39, no. 2 (2012): 371–81.

Another great trick to avoiding activities that don't add enough value to your life is using the twenty second rule: for activities you shouldn't be engaging in, or negative habits you want to break, add an element of difficulty, such as a twenty second roadblock to stand in the way of your starting the problem activity. For example, if you're trying to lessen your use of social media, delete the tempting apps from your phone, so it takes another twenty seconds to find your laptop to access them. By adding in an inconvenience, you'll be less likely to engage with that draining activity or habit.

On the other side of this is the perfectionist who seeks to tell another person how to do a job they both want done. "You aren't rinsing the dishes enough to go into the dishwasher!" How about showing some gratitude for them happily doing the dishes tonight? Offer suggestions, but only after appreciation! Who's right? Don't tell yourself or announce it to anyone. In the new 5D world, we lovingly appreciate all actions.

Another important tool mentioned in my book *Mastering Your 5D Self* is the information on the Five Dhyani Buddhas. The activation in the Five Dhyani Buddhas Meditation* allows you to personally activate your own Secret Ray Chakras.*

◆ How to Create a Portal Activation

Create your Galactic Council. This can include any of the beings you pray to. If you have no idea who you might be working with, I suggest you get your hands on the book *The Masters and their Retreats* by Mark L. Prophet and Elizabeth Clare Prophet. Some of the members of my team are Archangel Michael, St. Germain, Lord Maitreya, and Cuzco and Surya, along with the Mighty Blue Eagle! You may wish to add the ETs that may be part of your personal council, known or unknown. They can be Masters that are known ETs, like Sanat Kumara, or they might be 100 percent God Light Masters from Andromeda, for example.

Mastering Your 5D Self, chapter 3, pg 44.

A particularly significant assembly, alluded to earlier in this book, comprises the enigmatic beings known as the Secret-Ray Elohim. While their identities remain undisclosed, their influence is increasingly gaining prominence. One may invoke their presence for guidance in activating the energies emanating from higher dimensions. Engaging with the Elohim imparts a distinct advantage over commonplace habits and behaviors. Their ethereal influence acts as a catalyst, enhancing your spiritual mastery, and thereby manifesting your elevated expression, even in everyday life. With their assistance, the connection to Source is heightened, promising a profound and transformative journey.

Make your own list, then ask these Beings to serve as helpers and wayshowers for your spiritual work, assisting with various subjects you choose to master.

Here are some things you might ask your council to work with you on:

+ Eliminate the source of all evil in you, replacing it with your original divine blueprint.
+ You may ask this for children under age eighteen, or for your spouse.
+ Ask for your own highest vibrational data set to replace your current vibration. You might ask that this occur as gently and imperceptibly as possible, in dream time for example.
+ You might ask for decoy copies of yourself that can serve to obfuscate and confuse would-be attackers who may stand in the way of your success.

··· 12 ···

Holding Space for a Remarkable 5D Future

The threshold for everyone has elevated. Like boats in a harbor, the rising tide lifts all boats. The physical side of life, for many, wants stasis. Staying the same feels good, at least for a while, because it gives a sense of security and predictability. Yet, the mental and spiritual side of us needs more thinking time, more meditation time, and more simple quiet time alone and in nature.

Being open to life means having curiosity about everything. Make learning a priority. Make time for gradual transformation. Some of you will change effortlessly, in a split second. You may diligently contemplate every metamorphosis unfolding within you, in various facets of your being—physical alterations within your corporeal form, heightened mental acuity, augmented memory or memories pulled from the Akashic Records without knowing how or why, and expanded capacity of your intellect—while concurrently undergoing a spiritual transformation that surpasses any preconceived notions of your personal capability. What if everything worked out? An amazing way to manifest this is through the Golden Time Meditation.* Humans do not realize they already have the power to turn the tide of the life they have been living.

GOLDEN SHEETS

Have you ever found that your presence agitates some people? In group settings where there may be lots of interaction, people—including family members—may have entities and energies that are intimidated by your light. They don't necessarily intend to pick on you, their entities are simply looking for their lunch. Loosh is discussed further in Chapter 8. By wrapping yourself with the Golden Sheets, those individuals will not see or be intimidated by your light. The Golden Sheets' embracing energy will make you less of a threat to those challenged by your light. Then, when you go into any situation, for any reason, your light will not agitate others or make them uncomfortable around you.

When the Golden Sheets appeared in 2018, in a channeling session for the Ascension Institute members, we all were awed at their power, magnificence, and beauty. I honestly had forgotten about them, yet a very astute member was listening to a meditation where I had mentioned them, and asked for more information.

THE LORDS OF LIGHT SAID THIS DURING AN ASCENSION INSTITUTE TRAINING
December 16, 2021

This is the most important time to release this information. A person does not even need to understand to benefit. The Golden Sheets have gathered in groups all over the world. You might be asking, where are they from? They are directly from Source. They are sent as a direct answer to your direct request for ways to help others. You may put them on in the morning and keep asking for assistance, and we will provide our loving support.

Their power to impact this reality is significant. The Lords of Light have told us in a channeled session that they can be like wind shears. Wind shears can diffuse a hurricane! When the blue sphere beings left this part of the galaxy, the Golden Sheets came in as a new replacement of the blue sphere beings [see page 109]. They can take any shape and surround it. Although this information came in 2018, it was only released to the members of the Ascension Institute. Now, it is needed now more than ever.

Some of you may have heard of the blue sphere beings that were in our solar system with us for a long time, who left in 2018. I took this picture in a cave in France years earlier, when they were at my side while I was hiking alone in the Pyrenees. The blue sphere beings were a bit like the parent who shows up to a kid's party—everyone suddenly is on their best behavior around them. Bullies won't succeed while they are around.

I looked up "wind shear" on Wikipedia and found an interesting note from the internet game called *World of Warcraft* (my kids played this game): "Wind Shear: A quick blast of Ancestral Wind conceals

Blue Sphere Beings in a cave in the Pyrenees (circled).

the shaman, *lowering his or her threat to all enemies.*" Makes me think sometimes, that our children are getting "training" no matter what!

The Golden Sheets look like thin, gold, transparent sheets that are very wide. They have the capacity to adapt themselves to whatever shape is needed. They are beings of incredible light, and are imperceptible by many lower energies, which makes them great supporters, or tools, for humans to manage difficult situations where dense vibration prevails. As with every available support, lightworkers must ask for their help, calling them in by asking, "Golden Sheets, place your condom of light around me, my home, my city, etc. Then visualize them wrapping you or your physical abode, or situations and circumstances, with the Golden Sheets. Their vibration is at the etheric level.

In the Akashic Records
October 29, 2021

We, the Golden Sheets, have moved into your reality for the purpose of insulating you from the lower vibrations. Introduced to you by Maureen in 2018, you "set aside" this knowing until now, when it is important for others to know about and use. You "call in" the Golden Sheets as a name, then invoke the coverage area so that you see us a bit like shrink-wrap around a product or person. Because our energy is thin and filmy, we are not noticed by lower energies; however, we are extremely potent. This is a most appropriate time to release this new intel and encourage others to use us. We are directly from Source, sent as an answer to your direct request for ways to help others. Put it into the morning prayer and keep asking for our assistance, love, and support. That is all.

The Golden Sheets are mighty shields of protection for you and me. This is your first line of defense—and they are available to all. Think of them like bedsheets or plastic wrap. They can wrap around anything very tightly, and take the form or shape of whatever they are surrounding, elevating the vibration and transforming the experience of whatever they surround. They also serve to elevate the higher consciousness of any person surrounded by them, thus making it easier to choose their most evolved choice.

The Golden Sheets may also act as a filter. Just like moths are attracted to light, entities are attracted to our light. So, if there are any black magic or dark energies coming in, the Golden Sheets make your light invisible to those energies with an agenda contrary to yours.

There are stories of their effectiveness. In one case, a family facing difficulties was gloved—insulated, if you will—with the Golden Sheets. When the man of the home was working on the hot water radiator, a valve broke and 180-degree water came flooding out. Although he was burned, no skin was burned off his hand, which was highly unusual. Normally, this could have caused a severe burn.

When asking the Lords of Light about insulating someone or something, here's what they said:

Yes, you may. Let's say you are hosting family . . . put them [the Golden Sheets] around your home, yourself, the Christmas tree, the furnishings, yourself. Put a fresh Golden Sheets dispenser at the door to shrink-wrap everyone who comes through the door. It gives them a chance to level up. It changes their vibe at the etheric level for anyone who is not aware. You are aware. It doesn't change their free will. It simply levels them up at the etheric level. So that choices they make are more aligned with their divine self. They get clarity with their higher connections, even if they haven't earned it. Enough to make better choices.

They [the Golden Sheets] can help eliminate fear because fear is often a match for (fear) energy that is being broadcast. Fear is a messenger and fear is in the reality, originally as a messenger to assist people in seeing their lack of integrity between their thoughts and actions. The third kind of fear—that is coming from outside of humans and will not be able to affect you.

The Lords of Light want to remind you that all of these things are twenty-four-hour fixes, and you must be focused and clear. When you learn the MerKaBa, even the MerKaBa dissipates after about twenty-four to forty-eight hours, until it goes permanent. There are energies that will go permanent with your devotion, but it takes a while.

The Lords of Light want to be very clear about this. Many dark energies are leaving the planet . . . and may be causing upset and disruption as they leave, striking as hard as they can as they exit. When you call in the Golden Sheets, their presence initially is to prevent attacks on you, whether intended or accidental, whether reactionary or not. They also "up your game" at the etheric level, which filters down to the physical level.

THE LORDS OF LIGHT, CHANNELED MESSAGE
December 16, 2021

We are the Lords of Light, here to support your inquiry on the Golden Sheets. The Golden Sheets are magnificent beings of light. They are living plasma fields that can be called forth at your command. Their presence is an emanation of you using your God-spark power to ask for their presence to assign a work project and to achieve an outcome. This means that there were a limited number of Golden Sheets that were sent out into the reality to be programmed and used by humanity. Each time those Golden Sheets are assigned to a project, another one, like a blank piece of paper, takes its place. In this way you will find the ability to have an unlimited resource.

We ask you to not use this resource frivolously, but to use it with sincere purpose, claiming your God-spark and using them for the purpose of embracing or swaddling a situation or a person or a thing, like your home or your property. The purpose of the Golden Sheets, primarily, is to limit the visibility of your great light that would cause you to attract energy that is not of the light. This harboring energy that is not of the light is in the way of the full activation of the planetary plan of love and light.

Calling them forth means you get out of the way, and the energies that are not of the light cannot see you, but it allows Source and those higher beings who are helping to assist those that are of lesser value, to make new choices—to serve the light or to face extinction. The important thing is that you may use them around yourself, you may use them around others, you may use them around a physical object or an idea or concept that you are working on. This way you will cease to attract those who would have you fail. You will cease to attract those who are jealous of you or those who have misunderstandings about what is going on in the reality.

What we mean by this is there are individuals who sincerely believe certain things that a person must do in order to have what they would call eternal life. Those systems are no longer appropriate, even though they are still operational. And we make the metaphor that when Windows 98 went into the archives, they sent notices to everyone who had Windows 98 on their computers, saying it will no longer be serviced, there will no longer be answers to the questions you may have, or service bugs that might have cropped up in the software will not be fixed. So, in the same way, those beings who are not willing to serve the light are being retired, and then they are being faced with options to go into service to the light or not—it is their free-will choice. You are out of the way, and you are "out of harm's way."

Using the Golden Sheets in your home, you might think of them as Saran Wrap that is clear and gives no indication that it is hiding anything, but is more like a one-way mirror, so those that see in don't see anything unusual, but you will know your light is visible to those who have that capacity. So, you allow it to shrink-wrap or envelop the space you have defined, so that it is tightly sealed within the energy of the Golden Sheets. They are extremely malleable and can adapt to any shape and create a crystal clear shield that primarily serves to make your light invisible to those who would have you fail.

We will say to you that the Golden Sheets will serve to mitigate harmful effects. So, if you have the Golden Sheets around you and you are caught in a rainstorm without your umbrella, you might get wet but you won't get soaked like you might have. So, their influence in the 3D realm mitigates whatever it is that might be coming at you in 3D. If you were in a car situation where the car was headed for an accident, the Golden Sheets would allow what you would call in your world "a miracle" to occur. And either allow the energy to move into that 4th-Dimensional energy that they are holding for you, and then slide back out. So, you could literally slide through another vehicle instead of hitting it—raising your vibration in the process—because the vibrational shift that occurs is that they can slide or slide you into what you call 4th Dimension in order to not be a participant in a 3D collision. They might also soften the blow, so a major accident might turn into a minor accident.

We would encourage you to use the Golden Sheets on a regular basis without an agenda. In this way, the Golden Sheets can operate at their highest level. Your agenda may actually lower their capacity. You can see the Golden Sheets around your home and your property line every day. You might see a windstorm, and it might trigger you to do the Golden Sheets, but not out of fear, not out of the need for protection, but out of a place of "Oh, it's cold outside, I should grab a jacket."

There are many who will read this information and perhaps ignore it. We say to you—let them, you will benefit. Do not try to convince anyone. Let them try it and let them see what happens.

We encourage you to look upon this as a primary resource to get out of the way of any dark energy that might be around you or aimed at you. And, secondarily, it will serve to mitigate physical impacts, which will be a blessing as well.*

---

*The first time the Lords of Light came through with information about the Golden Sheets, the word they used to describe the envelopment of the Golden Sheets was *condom*. But with the connotation of the word, they began using the word *gloved*.

··· 13 ···

The 8D MerKaBa

The 8D MerKaBa takes advantage of the understanding of the Classic MerKaBa, also known as the seventeen-breath MerKaBa. The 8D MerKaBa integrates the original and authentic MerKaBa training, a truly phenomenal tool for ascension, as originally released by Drunvalo Melchizdek. As a certified facilitator, I have taught original, powerful Classic MerKaBa worldwide since 1994. This is a completely balanced form of meditation that repairs all aspects of the mental and emotional body, and helps heal the physical body.

To activate the 8D MerKaBa, I highly recommend you construct an icosidodecahedron before you begin this meditation (see the instructions in appendix 3).

Doing the Classic MerKaBa will help you heal and repair all aspects of your humanity. Drunvalo has said that if you can get the three star tetrahedrons perfect, you would become perfect in mind, body, and spirit. This is a self-healing tool that will assist in repairing anything that needs it. While looking at the MerKaBa fields of individuals who have activated their MerKaBas, I see that these "repairs" are real.

Because the MerKaBa seeks to balance the three lower bodies, one can reliably use this activated MerKaBa to clear blockages and open the heart. It is a centrifugal field that is impenetrable and allows for the heart to open and remain open, due to the "sealed field" effect. This means the heart can remain open even in difficult situations. This allows the individual to be in the 3D reality while expressing at a 5D level. This state allows for the fullest expression of unconditional love on the planet while interacting with those who are 3D.

This classic meditation allows one to use their mind and their heart *together*, achieving the state of consciousness called the MerKaBa. It invites the mind and the heart to participate in the evolution of consciousness, and as such is ideal for anyone with "monkey mind." Because the MerKaBa field creates balance at every level, it actively achieves connection with the 5th-Dimensional field of "no polarity," thus allowing a 5th-Dimensional aspect of the self to move into the 5th-Dimensional field, emphasizing the unconditional love aspect. This reinforces the open heart.

As a longtime facilitator of this sacred knowledge, I consider the Classic MerKaBa to be one of the easiest ways to achieve ascension! I have used the MerKaBa field in manifestation work, healing work, and as a resource for knowledge.

In addition, I've learned that it is a remarkable tool for healing, learning heart connection, and as a basis for expressing the 5th-Dimensional self. With an activated MerKaBa, one can become a true wisdom channel. It builds unity between the mind, body, and spirit, thus allowing for the full expression of the Higher Self through the presence of a perfectly harmonized vehicle of light—the unified field of personality in physical form.

Quite simply, it is remarkable. Incorrect practices can occur, and are due to not understanding the instruction clearly or learning the MerKaBa from a noncertified teacher. The original meditation was too good to retire, and my Higher Self told me to keep teaching it.

The MerKaBa Meditation* is a geometric symbol of creation and unity, as an expression of sacred geometry. (The term *Flower of Life* has often been interchanged for the actual MerKaBa, as well as the geometric shape.)

WHAT CAN YOU EXPECT FROM THIS MARVELOUS MEDITATION?

+ It mimics your Ascended Master self
+ It allows you to "wear the uniform" of your Ascended Master self
+ It allows you to connect with your Higher Self easily

+ It causes people to wake up
+ No one can lie to you while you wear your MerKaBa
+ It allows you to recognize who you really are, and that you do have the choice to come into a body! This means, no matter what you agreed to before entering a body, you may change your mind once you enter the freewill zone! You do choose the setup for your life!
+ You may learn that you are on a "special assignment"
+ You will learn that fulfilling your mission is dependent on *waking up*!
+ Realize that you do make contracts for fulfillment before coming in . . .
+ . . . and for after you arrive!
+ Learn that you may change contracts that are no longer working out
+ Learn that you do have a mission
+ Learn that you are part of the beings who have chosen to be here now
+ Learn that your efforts, no matter how insignificant, make a difference
+ Learn that your MerKaBa has a Manifestation field
+ Learn to balance male and female tetrahedrons and clear them

Translated literally from the Hebrew, the noun *merkavah* means "Chariot to ride in." It relates to the throne/chariot of God in prophetic visions, where a likeness of a man drives the chariot. The MerKaBa as we mean it here is a Body of Light, or Light Body. It is activated from a geometric field that exists around the body. Everyone has this field around them, as do planets, solar systems, and other living entities.

Sacred Geometry imparts strength and integrity. The spinning of counterrotating fields found throughout the cosmos is an accurate reflection of nature. In the Zohar, the mystical commentary on the Judaic Torah, there is a reference to the MerKaBa and the four wheels spinning "without turning."

The information we have today, both ancient and accurate, was already known at some level long before the MerKaBa became available to all of humanity—which means learning it is a *remembering* experience for humans. Once you have remembered the MerKaBa, you can choose to activate it daily until it becomes permanent.

The MerKaBa is also mentioned in the Old Testament, in Ezekiel 1:10. There is a popular spiritual, written by William L. Dawson, titled *Ezekiel Saw de Wheel*, which quotes from that section of the Bible. There are many versions of it on YouTube.

The actual throne on its chariot goes back to the first chapter of Ezekiel and his vision of a throne of glory that is a source of centuries-old mystical and visionary traditions. Some versions do not use the word *merkavah* when referring to the vehicle seen by Ezekiel, but it most certainly was this chariot that Ezekiel saw. This represents the entire star tetrahedron, filling, balancing, and spinning spheres around heart, creating centered energy.

The MerKaBa is a 5th-Dimensional garment that we remember and activate. It is not necessary to acquire it, as it is already there. In meditation, you will remember it! It is from the future, more advanced version of us. This, combined with the Christ Consciousness grid around the Earth, ensures our ascension. The addition of the 8D Activation allows you to connect with your star family.

With the addition of the 8D MerKaBa you will go beyond the speed of light to activate your 8D MerKaBa!

Let's start with the Classic MerKaBa. The first six breaths are the most complex, but don't be put off by this, just know that it gets easier. All seventeen breaths in this meditation rely on three things: a mudra, visualization or intention, and a particular way of inhaling and exhaling. The meditation is divided into four phases, with each phase containing only slightly different elements.

The first six breaths, which are the same with the exception of the mudra, have a very specialized way of ending the inhale, so we'll get to that in just a bit. First, we'll do the easy part and show you the mudras for the entire meditation. Phases 1, 2, and 3 represent three choices—all acceptable mudras—for "hands nested, thumbs touching."

The MerKaBa Meditation* can be broken into four phases. Each of the four phases involves a different kind of breath. In the first phase, practice deep, pranic breathing to inhale, exhale, and hold your breath. You are "holding" on empty. The second phase continues with deep, pranic breathing, but you no longer hold your breath. At the end of phase three, allow your breathing to become a little more shallow as you move into your heart. And finally, phase four is where you will activate your MerKaBa.

When you are instructed to put your eyes "in and up," do not do that until you hear the word "pulse." Like a child waiting to hear "go" at the beginning of a race starting with "ready, set, go!" please remember to wait until you hear the word "pulse" before looking "in and up, and then down."

Finally, please remember to always complete Breath Seventeen after Breath Sixteen—they must be done together.

◆ Preparation for the 8D MerKaBa Meditation

In order to prepare for the following exercise, you will need to create an icosidodecahedron 8D MerKaBa, as directed in appendix 3. (See pages 141 to 143.)

Begin in place where you feel safe and sacred, where you won't be disturbed for at least ten to fifteen minutes. If you have an altar, sitting in front of it is best, but sitting outside on the ground is just as holy. Any place you find safe and make sacred is appropriate. Sit, stand, or lie with your back straight. If sitting, either put your feet flat on the floor or sit in the lotus position. Using deep, pranic breathing, your belly should move in and out as you breathe through your nose.

The most important aspect of this meditation is to "be in your heart." Without this, your MerKaBa will be like a car without gas. It needs your love to power it up! So, allow yourself to feel your heart's energy using the following visualization. Think of holding a beloved child or pet in your arms, and feel the sensation of great love for this little one. This being isn't able to return your love in the same manner, so you have no expectation of this. Feel your unconditional love, and hear yourself telling this little one "I love you," followed by its name. Enjoy that wonderful feeling.

Phase 1

Breath 1

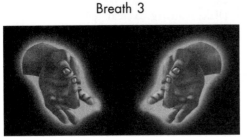

Breath 2

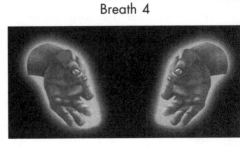

Breath 3

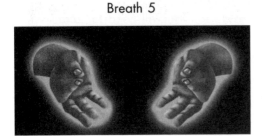

Breath 4

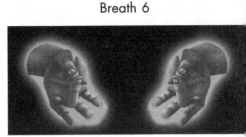

Breath 5

Breath 6

Now, allow the visual to fade while the feeling remains. You may name this feeling, such as "heart," "pink," "red," call it "love," or see it as the color green, as green is the color of the heart chakra. You can re-create this "great love for all of life" feeling anytime by mentally calling it forth by name and allowing the emotion of unconditional love to emanate from your heart.

The greater your capacity to embody unconditional love, the greater your results will be for your MerKaBa.

When moving from one breath to the next (for the first six breaths only), the "pulse" movement is the last thing you do before inhaling and changing mudras. "Pulse" invites an eye motion, not a head

Phase 2

Breath 7 through 13

Phase 3

Breath 14

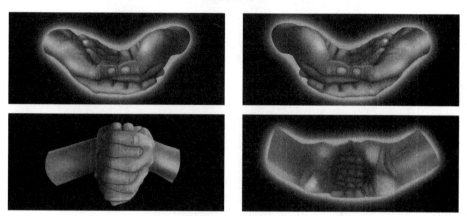

Above represents four choices, all acceptable mudras,
for "hands nested thumbs touching."

Phase 4

Breath 15, 16, and 17 choose the same mudra as you did for breath 14

motion—allow your eyes to move slightly inward, but not completely cross-eyed, then roll your eyes up as high as they will go, and then quickly look downward. This takes a little practice. Do this step slowly, moving your eyes in, up, and then down at the command of the word "pulse." These three movements can gradually be done more quickly, until you can comfortably do it faster and faster. Take your time here. This sequence of eye movements comes at the end of each of the first six breaths.

Begin the meditation with your next breath.

◈ 8D MerKaBa Meditation

Phase 1: Practice deep, pranic breathing to inhale,
exhale, and hold your breath.

✦ Breath One

Exhale a cleansing breath to begin.

Inhale using the first mudra, with thumb and first finger of each hand together.

Visualize the Sun tetrahedron around your body, filled with magnificent light.

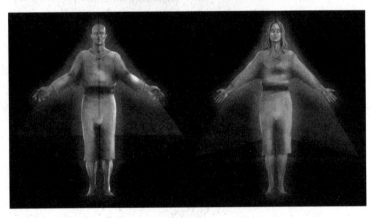

Exhale, visualizing the Earth tetrahedron around your body, filled with brilliant light.

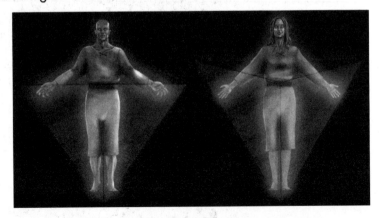

Hold your breath, visualizing the Earth tetrahedron, allowing any negativity to coalesce at its bottom, as shown below.

Pulse!—moving your eyes in, up, and then down in one smooth movement. Please remember to wait until after thinking the words "eyes in and up" before doing the eye movements. Finish the first six breaths with the eye movement at the word "pulse" simultaneously.

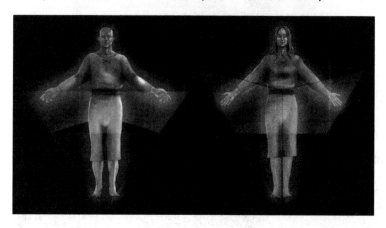

✦ Breath Two

Inhale using the second mudra, with thumb and second finger of each hand together.

Visualize the Sun tetrahedron around your body, filled with magnificent light.

Exhale, visualizing the Earth tetrahedron around your body, filled with brilliant light.

Hold your breath, visualizing the Earth tetrahedron, allowing any negativity to coalesce.

Pulse!—moving your eyes in, up, and then down in one smooth movement.

✦ Breath Three

Inhale using the third mudra, with thumb and third finger of each hand together.

Visualize the Sun tetrahedron around your body, filled with magnificent light.

Exhale, visualizing the Earth tetrahedron around your body, filled with brilliant light.

Hold your breath, visualizing the Earth tetrahedron, allowing any negativity to coalesce.

Pulse!—moving your eyes in, up, and then down in one smooth movement.

✦ Breath Four

Inhale using the fourth mudra, with thumb and fourth finger of each hand together.

Visualize the Sun tetrahedron around your body, filled with magnificent light.

Exhale, visualizing the Earth tetrahedron around your body, filled with brilliant light.

Hold your breath, visualizing the Earth tetrahedron, allowing any negativity to coalesce.

Pulse!—moving your eyes in, up, and then down in one smooth movement.

✦ Breath Five

Inhale, again using the first mudra, with thumb and first finger of each hand together.

Visualize the Sun tetrahedron around your body, filled with magnificent light.

Exhale, visualizing the Earth tetrahedron around your body, filled with brilliant light.

Hold your breath, visualizing the Earth tetrahedron, allowing any negativity to coalesce.

Pulse!—moving your eyes in, up, and then down in one smooth movement.

✦ Breath Six

Inhale, again using the second mudra, with thumb and second finger of each hand together.

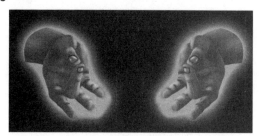

Visualize the Sun tetrahedron around your body, filled with magnificent light.

Exhale, visualizing the Earth tetrahedron around your body, filled with brilliant light.

Hold your breath, visualizing the Earth tetrahedron, allowing any negativity to coalesce.

Pulse!—moving your eyes in, up, and then down in one smooth movement.

Phase 2: Continue with deep, pranic breathing, but don't hold your breath. You will not be doing the "Pulse" anymore.

✦ Breath Seven

Inhale using the seventh mudra, with thumb and first two fingers together.

Visualize your pranic tube entering your body from both the crown and perineum, meeting in the center of your body behind your navel, and creating a sphere about the size of a grapefruit.

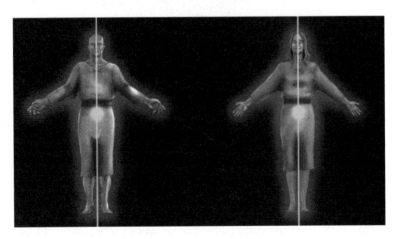

Exhale, visualizing the spheres filling with prana, allowing it to grow in size. Continue visualizing prana coming into this sphere until it has reached full size, about the size of a basketball.

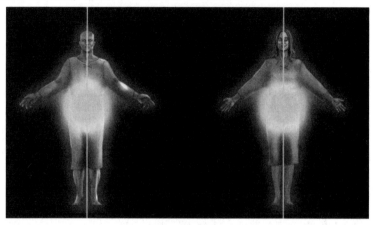

◆ **Breath Eight**

Inhale, again using the seventh mudra, with thumb and first two fingers together.

Visualize your pranic tube entering your body from both the crown and perineum, meeting in the center of your body behind your navel, and creating a sphere about the size of a grapefruit.

Exhale, visualizing the spheres filling with prana, allowing it to grow in size. Continue visualizing prana coming into this sphere until it has reached full size, about the size of a basketball.

✦ Breath Nine

Inhale, again using the seventh mudra, with thumb and first two fingers together.

Continue visualizing prana entering the sphere. You are "supercharging" the sphere with prana, making it very dense and brilliant.

Exhale, filling your sphere with prana, so it is very bright, like a full harvest moon.

✦ Breath Ten

Inhale, again using the seventh mudra, with thumb and first two fingers together.

Continue supercharging your sphere with prana. It will get very bright, like a sun ready to explode.

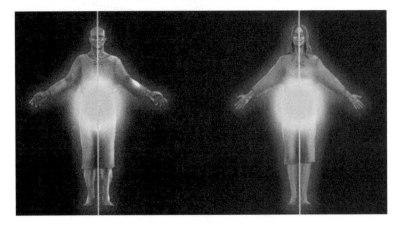

Exhale, forming a small hole with your lips and pushing a forced breath. Your sphere has instantly popped out to Vitruvian-Man-sized, a large golden sphere around your body.

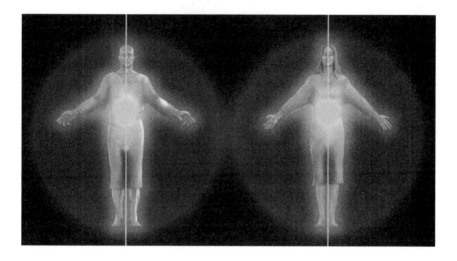

✦ Breath Eleven

Inhale, again using the seventh mudra, with thumb and first two fingers together.

You are now stabilizing your sphere as you breathe. Allow yourself to access more prana moving in from both directions.

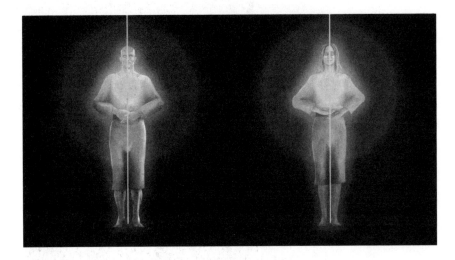

Exhale, forcing the breath through pursed lips, stabilizing the sphere around your body.

✦ Breath Twelve

Inhale, again using the seventh mudra, with thumb and first two fingers together.

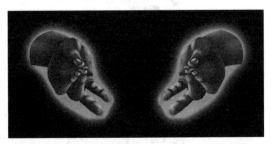

Exhale, forcing the breath through pursed lips, stabilizing the sphere around your body.

Inhale, allowing yourself to see more prana moving in from both directions.

Continue to breathe stabilizing prana into the sphere, forcing the exhale through pursed lips.

✦ Breath Thirteen

Inhale, again using the seventh mudra, with thumb and first two fingers together.

Inhale, allowing yourself to see more prana moving in from both directions.

Continue to breathe stabilizing prana into the sphere, forcing the exhale through pursed lips.

Phase 3: Allow your breathing to become a little shallower as you move into your heart.

✦ Breath Fourteen

Inhale, changing mudras. Beginning with hands nested, thumbs touching, allow the center of your spheres to move to your heart from your solar plexus.

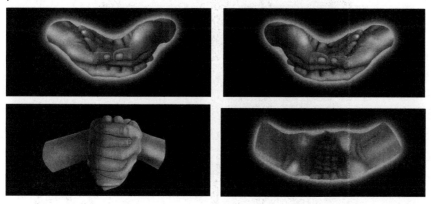

Visualize the entire field of light centered around your heart. Exhale, allowing yourself to feel your heart energy—that great love of all life. As you continue to feel love, allow your breathing to become more shallow. **Rest in your heart** a moment before moving on to the next phase.

Ask your Higher Self to show you how much you are loved. Let that feeling of love envelop you. You can ask your Higher Self this question anytime, and this feeling of love will return to you again and again. "Higher Self, show me how much I am loved."

Ask your Higher Self to practice your signals or symbols for "yes," "no," and "neutral."

Phase 4: Activating your MerKaBa.

✦ Breath Fifteen

Command: Spin equal speed

There are three star-tetrahedrons around the body:

The one moving to the left represents the **mental body.**

The one moving to the right represents the **emotional body**.

The one remaining stationary represents the **physical body**.

Inhale, visualizing the mental and emotional star-tetrahedrons spinning in opposite directions at equal speeds around the physical body star tetrahedron, which doesn't move.

Exhale a forced breath through pursed lips.

The spinning tetrahedrons are now moving at approximately one-third the speed of light.

✦ Breath Sixteen

Command: Spin 34 to the left, 21 to the right

Inhale, visualizing the mental and emotional star-tetrahedrons spinning — thirty-four times to the left, twenty-one times to the right — around the third star tetrahedron, which doesn't move.

Exhale a forced breath through pursed lips.

Instantly, the pranic field has created a large golden platter approximately fifty-five feet in diameter around your hips, and the tetrahedrons are now spinning in a Fibonacci ratio of approximately two-thirds the speed of light. The tetrahedrons equators are centered around your hips and your sphere is at your heart. Remember to always complete Breath Seventeen after Breath Sixteen — they must be done together.

✦ Breath Seventeen

Command: Spin Mental Body 9/10 the Speed of Light

Inhale, visualize that the tetrahedrons are now being stabilized by raising the speed of the mental body to nine tenths the speed of light keeping the phi ratio with the emotional body.

Remember, there are three star-tetrahedrons around the body:

The one moving to the left represents the **mental body**.

The one moving to the right represents the **emotional body**.

The one remaining stationary represents the **physical body**.

Exhale a forced breath through pursed lips.

Your tetrahedrons are now moving at the *speed of all life* and are tuned to 5th Dimension.

If you could see them, they would create a large golden platter.

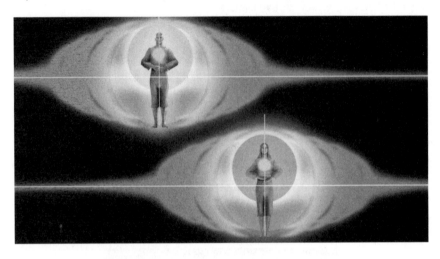

Continue breathing using the icosidodecahedron 8D MerKaBa you constructed, as directed in appendix 3.

◆ *Activation*

This activation will take your new 8D MerKaBa beyond the speed of light. Keep your newly constructed icosidodecahedron close by.

Inhale command: Equal speed of two whole icosidodecahedrons spinning around the third one, all sharing the same axis.

Exhale a forced breath through pursed lips.

Inhale command: Spin Mental Body **89, 55** causing each of the icosidodecahedrons to spin in opposite directions around the third one, all sharing the same axis to move into the phi ratio.

Exhale a forced breath through pursed lips.

Special note: Remember, there are three icosidodecahedron around the body. One moving to the left is the mental body, the one moving to the right is the emotional body, one remaining stationary represents the physical body. The physical icosidodecahedron does not spin, and remains stationary.

Activation (Keeping your newly constructed icosidodecahedron close by.)

Command: Activate! Intend the icosidodecahedron spinning to the left to move through the speed of light maintaining the phi ratio with the remaining spinning one!

Exhale a forced breath through pursed lips.

This activation will take your new 8D MerKaBa beyond the speed of light.

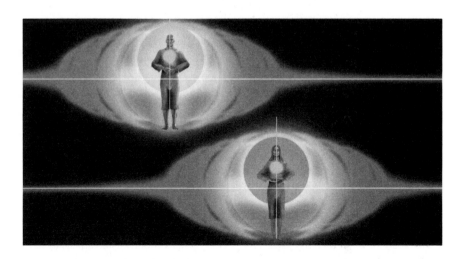

Conclusion

The 8D MerKaBa offers an expanded experience, and is a powerful transformational gift when used wisely. I recommend starting with the MerKaBa to begin expanding your awareness into the 5th Dimension before working with the 8D MerKaBa. Many of my close students practice both, as the 5D MerKaBa prepares your environment for the 5th Dimension, and the 8D MerKaBa is the next step in that progression.

After reading this book or engaging in the practices outlined, anticipate spontaneous bliss in your life. You'll gain knowledge when you need it, find humor in challenging situations, and experience greater balance, resulting in peace of mind, body, and soul as you embrace your best 5D life!

Bedtime Prayer

Updated August 31, 2023

I am getting a good rest and I am waking up well rested, no matter what the night holds. I claim that I am waking up in 5D. I am setting up an energetic Faraday cage around my bed, and around my body for the next twenty-four hours, to eliminate any EMF or other energies inappropriate for life.

I am entering a REVERSE AGING machine that is already set up for me. I am emerging younger; my new age is _____. I am pain free, disease free, negative energy free, and healthy each day. I am opening my pineal gland to distribute my pineal gland energies throughout my body in a torus formation—this helps me relax into the energies the Earth is going through.

I am my Ascended Master self, right here and now in the physical. I am Ascended Master [insert your name]. I am the version of me that is already ascended.

I now activate my Genesis Cells.

I command my Genesis Cells to activate NOW (repeat three times).

I now command my entire DNA system to support the activation of my Genesis Cells throughout all times and all dimensions and all of my selves.

I now command bolts of God's crystalline light to blaze in, through, and around my self-healing DNA strands, and to wake up and phase up to where I am to cleanse, heal, activate, and integrate them into my DNA structure, allowing them to expand and grow. This will speed up the self-healing process and allow them to serve me where I am. I now command my Higher Self to assist me in rearranging my molecules to harmonize with my new awareness and understanding of time and space. This allows me to shift dimensionally with grace and ease. This permits me to move my awareness beyond my current dimension, allow my focus in more than one dimension, and to remember my experiences. I let go and release all of my prior genetic programming. I command my Higher Self to locate the highest vibrational frequency my body has ever had; I command my Higher Self to energize and reattach it. I command my Higher Self to connect to my DNA and to each of my sixty-four codons that make up the full spectrum of my DNA, to increase their highest frequency. I open my heart to receive the highest DNA activation possible.

I now command my Higher Self assist me in rearranging my molecules to harmonize with my new awareness and understanding of time and space. This allows me to shift dimensionally with grace and ease. This permits me to move my awareness beyond my current dimension, allow my focus in more than one dimension, and to remember my experiences.

I am happy, healthy, wealthy, and wise. I am grateful for this great day, great opportunities, and great friends. I am grateful for every good thing coming my way!

Antidote for Planetary Retrogrades

ANTIDOTE FOR MERCURY RETROGRADE

I ask for clear communication, grace and ease with timing, and smooth operating equipment during this Mercury Retrograde.

I ask for all the benefits of this retrograde.

I further ask to antidote all the disadvantages of this retrograde.

◆ ◆ ◆

Do not do this prayer every day during an astrological Mercury Retrograde. This is a period for you to slow down, to find mistakes, and to breathe. Our need to always be busy will be frustrated if we try to move at our normal pace during a Mercury Retrograde. It's also great for equipment repairs.

ANTIDOTE FOR MARS RETROGRADE

I ask for a clear life review of boundaries, frustrations,
and old patterns that may need rejuvenating.
I also ask for patience, more me time, and slow deliberations
as I review my priorities, get more rest,
and exercise during this Mars Retrograde.

◆ ◆ ◆

What's a Mars Retrograde good for? It's good for all sorts of rethinking and reinventing. It impacts us for six weeks every two years. It is a "template" to set the stage for improving our direction, getting out of habits that no longer serve us, and choosing what to keep doing and what to change.

Mars retrograde invites major change. Change is hard for some. Work with it, and grow!

APPENDIX 3

Constructing an 8D MerKaBa Icosidodecahedron for Activating Your 8D MerKaBa

This process can take time, and your patience will pay off. To make this icosidodecahedron, you will need to construct thirty crosses in the Phi ratio. These crosses together will create an icosidodecahedron. This construction produces an icosahedron and a dodecahedron in Phi relative to one another.

There are four stages for building this shape:

1. Assembling the Right Tools
2. Preparing the Components
3. Creating the Crosses
4. Construction

Stage 1. Assembling the Right Tools

+ Clear ruler that measures inches in tenths (five divisions in each half inch)
+ Low-melt glue gun and glue sticks
+ Forty 3/8" or 3/16" dowels (or branches!). You can get dowels from an art supply store, like Michaels.
+ Garden pruning shears big enough to cut the dowels or sticks

✦ Paper of any kind—if you get glue on your fingers, immediately touch it to the paper, which will take the glue and heat from your finger.

Stage 2. Preparing the Components

Cut thirty sticks at 5.5"

Cut sixty sticks at 1.5"

Stage 3. Creating the Crosses

Glue a shorter stick to the center of each long stick

Getting to Phi: 5.5 (represented by the long stick) divided by 1.618 (Phi) is 3.40 (total length of the short side). You will need two short sticks on either side to make a Phi cross.

The shorter sticks need to be 1.5" long because the glue and center stick take up the remaining distance—the width of the long stick adds

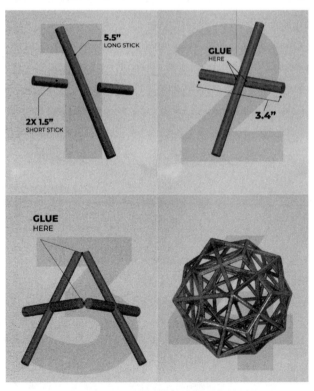

to the overall length of the shorter piece. Be very careful measuring your sticks, because if they're not precise the pieces will not fit together. The easiest way to do this is to draw on a piece of cardboard the two lengths you are cutting (5.5" and 1.5"). One length is 5.5, and for each one of those you will have two 1.5" sticks. You can make your icosidodecahedron any size, but we found this size to be the easiest.

Stage 4. Construction

Using the glue gun, construct all the crosses touching each other. It is useful to have another person help with this as you go.

Glue them together, meeting **short cross side** to **short cross side**, long cross side to long cross side:

Allow the connections to curve into one another, bending slightly toward a center.

**Congratulations, you are now ready
to activate your 8D MerKaBa!**

Index